DARK DAYS

Screenplay
by
Jodie Jones

ISBN-13:
978-1492159483

ISBN-10:
1492159484

Published by: Jodie Jones

jodiejones09@gmail.com

EXT. ROAD, BORDERLANDS - DAY

The lone road carving through the BorderLands woods has only one occupant, a RED 1979 SUBURBAN, parked across both lanes.

JUNIOR, 28, comfortably sunbathes on the roof, his shirt unbutton exposing his torso. He has good features, but hard, an almost compassionate look, but we know better, the 28 year old's an asshole. This era's Uday Hussein.

                    JUNIOR
          I'm bored Dykes. Find me the poachers. I'm in need
          of some action.

DYKES, 30s, in the driver's seat wearing the Guardian's uniform, grabs the walkie.

                    DYKES
          Give me a sit-rep Horace. We're getting anxious
          here.

EXT. WOODS, BORDERLANDS - DAY

In the woods sitting on their Red motorcycles are HORACE, 30s, and BRICK, 25. They too wear the Guardian's soldier uniform: mainly all black with shades and trimmings of red, more like a paramilitary uniform from a battlefield in Serbia or Columbia. But, in this post war age, you have already learned to respect and fear that uniform. They're more Nazi SS than that of a regular soldier or policeman.

                    HORACE
          You still got 'em?

Brick's tracking with his binoculars.

                    BRICK
          Yeah.

Horace presses down on the walkie.

                    HORACE
          We've found them.

                    DYKES (O.S.)
               (on walkie)
          Flush 'em to us.

Horace pockets the walkie into one of his saddle bags.

                    HORACE
          Junior's in his mood to play. Let's get this going.

Brick pockets his binoculars into his saddle bag.

> BRICK
> What's wrong with that guy?

> HORACE
> He's a sadistic psychotic son of a bitch. But, he's one
> of our bosses.

> BRICK
> We seem to have a lot of those these days.

> HORACE
> Yep.

They don their red, black tinted motorcycle helmets and KICK START their bikes TO
LIFE. Brick COCKS his SIG SAUER and places the gun back in its holster attached to
his handle bar.

EXT. WOODS, BORDERLANDS - DAY

Traveling through the scarred wooded terrain of the BorderLands...

KYRA, 13, our girl narrator.

> KYRA (V.O.)
> There were varying opinions on what finally started
> the war...

Except for the various discarded litter, the few left behind junk, one could mistakenly
think that we're in yesterday's world. But, we're not...

> KYRA (V.O.) (CONT'D)
> The world economies crashing, the famines, the
> widespread plagues, old rivalries finally settling their
> scores...

We pass the animal carcass, travel up the small sloped hill...

> KYRA (V.O.) (CONT'D)
> Whatever the reason, bombs rained from the sky,
> armies battled on multiple fronts, nations were
> destroyed, old powers ravaged...

A FORCE OF NOISE BLASTS into our peaceful woods, GROWING LOUDER,
heading our way...followed by GUNSHOTS!

Hell on Earth.

A camouflaged spray painted pickup truck launches into our scene, catching air as it ramps the crest and CRASHES DOWN on the sloped hill RAMPAGING pass us.

TWIN MOTORIZED NOISES holds our attention on the slope. The two Red motorcycles ramp the crest of the hill, charging after the speeding truck.

INT. ROMAN'S PICK UP TRUCK - CONTINUOUS

ROMAN, 31, does everything in his power to keep control of the truck. The ex soldier has a death lock grip on the wheel.

ROMAN
Hold on! Stay with me Miller!

His buddy, MILLER, bleeding profusely from the gunshot wound, is slowly dying. It doesn't look good.

EXT. WOODS, BORDERLANDS - CONTINUOUS

Roman's truck SMASHES through the smaller trees and foliage, expertly maneuvers between and around the larger ones all the while hauling ass and grinding up dirt. The tarp covered cargo in the bed bump and bounce but miraculously remain latched and tied in the back.

The two Red motorcycles match the truck's every move and are gaining ground. Horace and Brick are impressive, they'll be tough to outrun.

INT. ROMAN'S PICK UP TRUCK - CONTINUOUS

Miller tries to stop the blood from gushing out of his chest. He weakly slides the pistol over the seat.

MILLER
(struggling)
Take it. Don't let them kill us both.

ROMAN
You're not going to die, damn it! Hold on!

Roman cuts the truck hard to the left! The motorcycles gaining. He grabs the pistol from the seat and with one swift motion pops the cylinder out--no bullets!

ROMAN (CONT'D)
Bullets!

                              MILLER
                            (struggling)
                        Check the box.

Roman reaches for the ammo tin box on the dash, flings it open to find...only ONE
BULLET left.

                              ROMAN
                    Shit.

EXT. WOODS, BORDERLANDS - CONTINUOUS

Horace easily steers his motorcycle with one hand as he slips his GLOCK from the
holster attached to where the speedometer should be. Brick already has his SIG SAUER
out and FIRES! The bullet EXPLODES the back windshield of the truck!

Roman's evasive maneuvers through the trees separates them enough from the oncoming
motorcycles. BAM! Another shot fired, but this one misses. The pick up truck
rampages on, the motorcycles now having a harder time keeping up.

EXT. ROAD, BORDERLANDS - CONTINUOUS

The Red Suburban flies along the lone road with the chase off road in the woods.

INT. RED 1979 SUBURBAN - CONTINUOUS

Junior LOADS the last magazine into his UZI. He takes a wild, good for nothing
SPRAY OF SHOTS in the general direction of the racing pick up truck in the woods.
The maniac LAUGHS. Dykes drives.

                              DYKES
                         (more to himself)
                        Wasting bullets.

Junior doesn't hear him, he's in his own crazy world.

                              JUNIOR
                      Off road it! Off road it!

Dykes cuts the Suburban hard off the road.

EXT. WOODS, BORDERLANDS - CONTINUOUS

The Red Suburban CRASHES THROUGH and joins the party! The motorcycles veer off
to the side allowing Dykes to race the Suburban up closer to Roman's pick up truck.

INT. ROMAN'S PICK UP TRUCK - CONTINUOUS

Roman bounces off his seat as the truck GRINDS HARDER through the terrain. Miller is COUGHING UP blood, his limp body rattling all inside the cab.

EXT. WOODS, BORDERLANDS - CONTINUOUS

The Red Suburban destroys everything in its path, the indestructible force easily makes its way to the bed of Roman's truck, but instead of slamming into it, Dykes expertly cuts along side allowing the crazy ass Junior to hang out the passenger side window and UNLEASH A FURY OF BULLETS!

INT. ROMAN'S PICK UP TRUCK - CONTINUOUS

Roman cuts away, but the Suburban is attached to its side.

> ROMAN
>
> Hold on!

He cuts hard, SLAMMING into the Red Suburban's front temporarily knocking the Red beast from its path. The Suburban falls behind the pick up.

INT. RED 1979 SUBURBAN - CONTINUOUS

> JUNIOR
>
> Other side! Other side!

Junior jumps to the back seat, readies his UZI while hanging out the window behind Dykes.

> JUNIOR (CONT'D)
> RIGHT UP TO THEM!

Dykes JAMS the pedal to the floor. Roman can't shake them. Roman does everything he can do, but the Suburban sticks with them, inching ever closer up along the pick up's passenger side.

> DYKES
> (more to himself)
> Wait...wait...

Junior doesn't. He UNLEASHES A FURIOUS VOLLEY OF BULLETS.

> DYKES (CONT'D)
>
> Shit!

Dykes SLAMS the accelerator to the floor harder.

INT. ROMAN'S PICK UP TRUCK - CONTINUOUS

PING PING PING CRASH!!! The bullets rain down on the pick up truck, EATING UP everything metal and glass in its path. Roman can't do anything.

> ROMAN
> Get down Miller! Get down!

Miller doesn't respond. Blood is everywhere. Is he dead? It doesn't matter-BAM!-SPLAT! A stream of Junior's bullets RAVAGE the truck with the tail end bullet finally HITTING its mark--Miller's head! Blood, scar tissue and brain EXPLODE inside the cab of the truck. Roman doesn't have time to think on it, he SLAMS on the brakes!

EXT. WOODS, BORDERLANDS - CONTINUOUS

The Red Suburban flies pass, almost losing control and almost tossing Junior out the window. Dykes SLAMS on the brakes. The motorcycles RACE PASS both stopping vehicles.

Roman JAMS DOWN the accelerator, fishtails his truck 180 around, races back the other way! Dykes copies Roman's move, but the massive Red Suburban takes longer giving Roman a better head start. The motorcycles ROAR back alongside the Suburban.

INT. RED 1979 SUBURBAN - CONTINUOUS

> JUNIOR
> (to Horace and Brick)
> FORCE THEM TO THE MINEFIELD! THE
> MINEFIELD!

> DYKES
> (more to himself)
> They can't hear you.

> JUNIOR
> (to Dykes)
> Force them to the minefield!

Junior checks his UZI clips.

> JUNIOR (CONT'D)
> Shit! I'm out.

EXT. WOODS, BORDERLANDS - CONTINUOUS

The Red Suburban and two motorcycles force and persuade the path of Roman towards their minefield. The valuable weapons of the motorcycles racing ahead and alongside the truck, with intermediate SHOTS FIRED to guide their prey, allows the Red Suburban to force Roman straight into the minefield.

EXT. MINEFIELD, BORDERLANDS - CONTINUOUS

The MINEFIELD. A stretch of terrain planted and littered with dangerous junk: scrap metal, massive spikes, barbwire, broken concrete slabs, old discarded vehicle parts with everything from 18 wheeler axles to bulldozer engines to Cadillac grills and more.

EXT. EDGE OF MINEFIELD, BORDERLANDS - CONTINUOUS

Dykes SKID STOPS the Red Suburban at the edge of the minefield. The two motorcycles ease their way up to a stop, flanking each side of the Red beast.

EXT. MINEFIELD, BORDERLANDS - CONTINUOUS

Roman's in too deep. His truck is out of control as he tries to slalom his way through the minefield. BANG! CLANG! It's getting worse, but screw it, he doesn't slow down. He cuts, dodges, even runs over junk. BAM! Slams into more shit.

POP! A rebarb infested slab of concrete draws first blood by DEMOLISHING Roman's front right side tire! The truck loses its balance-SLAM! Roman crashes into a rusted out half trailer! The truck catches air, rotates, flies sideways-BAM!-CRASH!-SLAMS into the ground EXPLODING earth all around it! The truck SLIDES another 30 yards on its side, the cargo broken free from its ropes and latches, is thrown out leaving a trail of damaged goods behind.

EXT. EDGE OF MINEFIELD, BORDERLANDS - CONTINUOUS

Junior and his Guardian soldiers, Dykes, Brick, and Horace, all stand looking down the minefield to the ravaged truck and its trail of destruction.

> KYRA (V.O.)
> But, I'm not here to talk about the war. Instead, I'm here to tell you about the aftermath, the time when the world,..

We look at each of the four men, starting with Junior as...

> KYRA (V.O.) (CONT'D)
> ..weary from the long fight, was struggling to get back on its feet.

EXT. MINEFIELD, BORDERLANDS - CONTINUOUS

The four men walk the minefield coming upon the trail of cargo from Roman's truck: a gas drum, a small generator, a large ice chest, camping essentials, and a ripped open military green duffel bag of clothes.

Junior takes a folded map from inside the duffel bag, opens the giant terrain map: a magnified portion of what use to be southeast Texas and southwest Louisiana. The BLUE markings are stalking the BROWN markings on the map like two submarines in a dogfight.

Junior's impressed. He sees what they have been stalking, two dead deer lay broken, close to the truck.

                         DYKES
          They're hunters, Junior.

                         JUNIOR
          Illegal hunters.

The men reach the truck. Miller's dead body is the only one left in the cab. Junior sees a backpack close, opens it to find a stack of papers inside.

                         JUNIOR (CONT'D)
               (flipping through)
          Miramar hunting licenses, weapons licenses, travel
          documents, authorized issued gas, Miramar gas paper
          card...
               (flips through the rest)
          Huh.

                         DYKES
          Looks like they were legal.

                         JUNIOR
               (smiles)
          According to the City-State of Miramar, not us.

Junior knows that's bullshit and it amuses him greatly, he gives off that maniacal laugh of his.

                         JUNIOR (CONT'D)
          Oh, well. My mistake.
               (laughs harder)

                         HORACE
          Can't find the driver.

Like a monkey in a jungle flying from one vine to the next, Junior's brain now completely latches onto this new, exciting, news.

                    JUNIOR
        Whoo Hoo! The hunt's still on! Find him! Horace,
        Brick, on your bikes! Dykes on foot! GO GO GO!

The men follow their orders. The hunt is on for Roman. Dykes takes out his two 9mm
pistols, lob throws one to Junior as he runs after the remaining hunter. Horace and Brick
race back to their bikes. Junior stays, pistol now in hand, looks over the spilled
cargo...then the two killed deer.

                    JUNIOR (CONT'D)
        Looks like we're having deer steak tonight boys!

EXT. OPPOSITE EDGE OF MINEFIELD, BORDERLANDS - CONTINUOUS

Roman runs for his life. The motorcycles COME TO LIFE in the short distance behind
him. He zig zags through and out of the minefield.

EXT. WOODS, BORDERLANDS - CONTINUOUS

Horace and Brick have flown around the outer edge of the minefield and spot Roman
running for his life.

Roman cuts across, jumps, veers, does everything to evade the oncoming bikes. He
SKID SLIDES down a slope, finds cover, slides into third! Covered in foliage, Roman
tries to CATCH HIS BREATH, gain his composure.

On foot, Dykes appears on the crest of the slope, stops, looks around...Roman remains
still, breathless...Horace appears on his bike next to Dykes...Horace GUNS the bike
away. Dykes runs away in the opposite direction.

Roman springs into action, hauls ass. We stay with him as he finds more cover, crouches
down, BREATHING HARD...CRACK! Tree bark SPLINTERS right by his head!
Dykes aims again from his close position! Roman runs.

Horace flies his motorcycle onto Roman's six, gaining on him. Roman runs into the
slalom course of trees! It works! Horace has a difficult time following on his
motorcycle.

Brick APPEARS out of nowhere! Skid stops then effortlessly step jumps off his
motorcycle in a full on run! By sure instinct, Roman twirls and FIRES his last bullet,
SLICING the side of Brick's throat! Brick SLAMS to the ground, desperately trying to
GASP more air through his bloody mess...his gasping STOPS.

Roman pauses for a fraction of a second--he's forced into action as Horace appears, his
motorcycle GUNNING right for him. Dykes too emerges running on foot. Dykes FIRES
his 9mm in the close distance running after the fleeing Roman.

                         ROMAN
                 They're everywhere.

CRACK! Splinters brush Roman's face, but remains on his running feet. He blindly runs
through the thick brush...can see the road up ahead! Roman turns back to check his
six...here comes Horace's motorcycle! Shit!

A low hanging branch, like a miracle, produces itself to Roman down the slope, heading
towards the road. He charges right for it. Horace's motorcycle GAINS on him, his Glock
out. Roman leaps for the branch, SMACKS right into it and holds on as the propelled
force swings the branch out. Roman lets go, drop sliding down at the exact moment,
WHIPPING the branch back!

The awesome force NAILS Horace smack dead in the chest, throwing him off his bike!
The speeding, riderless motorcycle flies through the woods down the slope, not stopping!

EXT. ROAD, BORDERLANDS - CONTINUOUS

The riderless motorcycle hits the roadside ditch and LAUNCH RAMPS over the road,
CRASHING DOWN on the other side ditch!

EXT. WOODS, BORDERLANDS - CONTINUOUS

Roman stares down the now free motorcycle.

                         ROMAN
                 My ride outta here.

He makes a mad last dash for it. Still chasing on foot, Dykes FIRES another shot that
misses.

EXT. ROAD, BORDERLANDS - CONTINUOUS

Roman BREAKS through the brush, then stumbles down the slope, but miraculously is
back on his feet.

We HEAR the Red Suburban racing on the road towards us but can't see it yet. Roman
reaches his new crashed motorcycle and desperately tries to KICK START it to life...

The Red Suburban appears in the distance, Roman knows it's now or never, still trying to
KICK START the battered bike to life.

INT. RED 1979 SUBURBAN - CONTINUOUS

Junior clearly sees the Hunter unsuccessfully trying to bring the motorcycle to life. He
tastes his kill, smiles, aims his 9mm out the window as he drives.

EXT. ROAD, BORDERLANDS - CONTINUOUS

                    ROMAN
          Come on!

SHOTS FIRED! Junior hangs out the window firing his 9mm while still handling the on coming Red Suburban.

Roman's motorcycle COUGHS TO LIFE! He PEELS OUT just as the suburban SCREECHES to a stop on the road not 20 yards away. Junior is already out FIRING at the now escaping Roman on the motorcycle.

Roman flies the bike off road into the wooded terrain on the opposite side of the road. Junior run chases after him EMPTYING his 9mm clip.

The running Dykes BREAKS through the brush, skid slides the roadside ditch to a stop on the road, looks at Junior.

A woozy Horace stumble runs his way from the woods to the road too.

Now, all three stand on the road watching Roman disappear into the woods.

                    JUNIOR
          After them!

But, nobody moves.

EXT. WOODS, OUTLANDS BORDER - DAY

Roman races his motorcycle up to the unofficial border of the Outlands territory: crumbled stoned wall in spots, ancient strung along barbwire, and anything else possible to completely indicate you're entering into another region.

The unofficial "wall" barrier border stretches as far as the eye can see to the left and the right.

Roman looks back through the woods, down to the road where the three men still stand. They aren't giving chase anymore. Roman KICKS it into gear and maneuvers his way through the "barrier".

He hops the motorcycle over the last hurdle and lands on a crudely makeshift, spray painted sign cracking it in half. Roman doesn't notice as he races off further into this territory.

We PAN DOWN to read the now cracked sign: OUTLANDS TERRITORY KEEP OUT

EXT. ROAD, BORDERLANDS - DAY

> JUNIOR
> You bitches just gonna stand here?

> DYKES
> OutLand Territory.

> HORACE
> Dwellers. I hate fucking Dwellers.

> JUNIOR
> You two ass holes are afraid of a bunch of dirty
> rubble leachers? Fuckin' pathetic.

> DYKES
> No matter. They're going to slice that Hunter to
> pieces anyway.

> JUNIOR
> Where's Brick?

> DYKES
> Didn't make it.

Junior SPIKES his empty 9mm onto the road, madman crazy.

> JUNIOR
> You two find your own way back.

> HORACE
> How?

> JUNIOR
> Figure it out.

With that, Junior gets back to the Red Suburban, PEELS OUT and AWAY leaving Dykes
and Horace staring off into the woods towards the OutLands on the road.

> HORACE
> Fucking hate Dwellers.

> DYKES
> Mmmm, hmmm.

FADE OUT:

FADE IN:

EXT. OUTSKIRTS OF THE CITY-STATE SIDEON'S CENTER TOWN - DAY

> KYRA (V.O.)
> Those who remained longed for the chaos and fear to
> end.

Scattered pedestrians, traveling to and from the wall surrounded City-State with their
crates, bags, boxes, and the such.

> KYRA (V.O.) (CONT'D)
> Safety, structure, a sense of hope became their
> priorities.

A motorcycle appears on the horizon, driving towards Sideon and its Center Town.

> KYRA (V.O.) (CONT'D)
> Unfortunately, this led to the rise of Tyrants.

POLICE MAYOR SYRON, 50s, fury incarnate, the big bad Boss, rides his Red
motorcycle pass Sideon's gates without any Guardian soldier objecting and into town
with not a care in the world. Syron is more Pablo Escobar than General Patton.

> KYRA (V.O.) (CONT'D)
> A time where they and their soldiers controlled their
> City-States with brutality and hate. A time we know
> as The Age of the Warlords.

EXT. THE CITY-STATE SIDEON'S CENTER TOWN - DAY

Syron rides pass us and we stay on the...

DILAPIDATED BRICK WALL. A red and black frayed and torn "UNCLE SAM"
poster of Sideon's War Lord, Police Mayor Syron. Syron points at you. The poster says:
'THE CITY-STATE OF SIDEON: THE IRON FIST IS WATCHING YOU'. 'UNITY
AND JUSTICE FOR ALL'.

EXT. BARTER EXCHANGE, ENTRANCE/EXIT, SIDEON - DAY

Traders are checked entering the razor wired topped tin fenced-in grounds. Ones exiting,
however, are being scrutinized and checked, not unlike the old baggage check-in lines at
the airport. Guardian Soldiers inspect every patron for illegal contraband. Bicycles,
carts, foot traffic people, not a vehicle in sight.

Near the entrance is a makeshift stage with three propagandized banners hanging from
high: one a refined portrait of Police Mayor Syron, the middle one of Syron's political
arm, the 2nd Front Party emblem, and the third the symbol for the City-State of Sideon.
The PREACHERMAN, with bullhorn, sermons from the stage.

                    PREACHERMAN
          Give thanks to the Almighty for the security and
          peace provided to us by our very own Police Mayor
          Syron! Sideon has flourished, the 2nd Front Party
          solidified, our new allegiance and treaty between us
          and the City-State of Miramar. Police Mayor Syron
          has ensured our strong growth and our ironclad
          peace! Together we are stronger than apart! Give
          thanks to our leader!

The crowd goes about their business of their day, ignoring the sermon. Same ole same
ole, this happens everyday.

                    PREACHERMAN (CONT'D)
          Sideon business. The curfew is still in effect until
          further notice. This is for your protection as the
          Guardian soldiers continue to weed out our City-State
          terrorists threatening the peace. Until this problem is
          eradicated, anyone caught out past curfew will be
          treated as an enemy combatant against Sideon.

Syron rides pass and we stay with him...

EXT. BARTER EXCHANGE, TIN WALL FENCE, SIDEON - DAY

...as his motorcycle rides up to Junior and the Red Suburban parked near a section of the
razor wired tin fence of the Barter Exchange.

Syron sees the damaged to the Red Suburban, immediately hops of his bike. He walks in
and around for a closer inspection.

                    POLICE MAYOR SYRON
          Son of a bitch.

                    JUNIOR
               (trying to save himself)
          Hunters. One dead, one unaccounted for.

Syron turns on him swiftly, violently choke SLAMS Junior against the Suburban.

                    POLICE MAYOR SYRON
               (eerily calm)
          Never take my vehicle out again.

Junior strugglingly nods.

Next time I see it, it'll be fixed. Want it good as new.

Syron releases Junior. Junior rubs his throat, but doesn't dare cough.

                    JUNIOR
               (hoarse)
          Yes, sir.

                    POLICE MAYOR SYRON
          Where's Ray?

                    JUNIOR
          Hasn't returned yet.

                    POLICE MAYOR SYRON
          Tell me about the two you tracked.

                    JUNIOR
          They had City-State Miramar issued licenses and gas.

Syron tightens his face, looks off.

                    POLICE MAYOR SYRON
               (more to himself)
          Goddamn Miramar. They think they can issue
          permits on *my lands*?

                    JUNIOR
          Technically, those woods are-

                    POLICE MAYOR SYRON
               (turns on Junior)
          Don't you finish that statement if you know what's
          good for you. Fuck that little weak ass City-State.
          Treaty or not.
               (looks off)
          Those our my lands, I say who gets to hunt on them.
          This Miramar...trying to disrupt my kingdom
               (back to Junior)
          Our kingdom.

                    JUNIOR
          What should we do?

                    POLICE MAYOR SYRON
          Clean 'em out before they think they're big enough to
          even challenge me. But, that's a problem for
          tomorrow. Tighten up the Guardian patrol, that's
          what we're focused on today.

                         JUNIOR
          Yes, sir.

                    POLICE MAYOR SYRON
          Tell me about this Hunter.
                    (off Junior's look)
          The one *you let* escape!

                         JUNIOR
          He, uh, went into the OutLands.

                    POLICE MAYOR SYRON
          You better pray he doesn't survive it in there. That's
          all I need is a defiant hero for the peasants.

He stares down Junior...then Syron walks off.

                    POLICE MAYOR SYRON (CONT'D)
          Kill two birds, Junior, go find Ray.

For the first time we see the brazen Junior look a bit nervous and unsure...

                         JUNIOR
          Shit.

EXT. OUTLANDS - DAY

Roman's motorcycle sputters out of gas in the rubble foliage overgrown mess of what
used to be civilization's neighborhood a decade ago. He drops the bike and sits on a
concrete slab to catch his wits and, more importantly, his sanity.

He checks his empty gun, his empty pockets...everything lost back at the truck. He drops
his head.

                         ROMAN
          I'm sorry Miller.

RUMBLINGS! Roman jerks his head up! Movement in his vicinity. Blurs of bodies run
flash in the foreground! Roman looks too late to see. Every time he looks one way, flash
blur of a body crosses in the foreground from the other way.

Roman senses trouble. We can feel that these blurs are encircling Roman like predators on a helpless prey. The blurs seem to be advancing closer and closer on Roman and he can't pinpoint where they are. Fuck it!

Roman bolts up, CRASH runs through the foliage to escape!

EXT. ABANDONED SUPERMARKET RUBBLE BUILDING, OUTLANDS - DAY

Roman finds himself in a large supermarket parking lot now being taken over by nature. A still standing carcass of a once supermarket building at its end. Roman runs to it.

The blurs CRASH THROUGH the surrounding foliage, converging on their prey, Roman!

> ROMAN
>
> What the...?

Roman briefly sees what they are, but turns his attention on reaching the supermarket.

The blurs look like humans, and they are, but years of abandonment, mob jungle like living and rule, find or kill what you can eating, even people, deplorable unsanitary living conditions in the heart of the direct missile and bomb hits from the long ago war of once civilized cities have turned these people into diseased ridden, beyond dirty, almost sub human like entities.

The WAR CRY ERUPTS from Roman's pursuers. They won't catch him.

> ROMAN (CONT'D)
>
> It's a trap.

They want him to go into the supermarket. Roman tries for another out. There is none. It's either chance it inside the carcass building or chance it against these crude weapon wielding crazies.

> ROMAN (CONT'D)
>
> No choice.

Roman scampers inside and disappears. The predators run to a walk, slowly gather while converging on the supermarket. They are women and men. They have everything from spiked pipes to chains to barbwire covered clubs and more. And they have a thirst for more blood.

MANUS, a giant of man, emerges to the front. The leader.

> MANUS
> WE HAVE A TRESPASSER! AND WHAT DO
> WE DO WITH TRESPASSERS!?!

The group, in unison, retort with a LOUD, SHORT BARK GRUNT! Manus lowers and points his multiple spiked rebarb spear forward.

                    MANUS (CONT'D)
          ONWARD!

Manus and his group casually walk towards the supermarket and their trespassing prey.

INT. ABANDONED SUPERMARKET RUBBLE BUILDING, OUTLANDS - DAY

Roman scrambles through the trash and decay of the once vibrant supermarket. He hops over a battered checkout counter and finds himself trapped with a pile of counters and shelves thwarting his advance. He looks back to see Manus and his group of crazies reach the front of the store.

Roman looks for a way out...there is none.

                    ROMAN
          Shit.

EXT. ABANDONED SUPERMARKET RUBBLE BUILDING, OUTLANDS - DAY

Manus climbs through the paneless bay window. His band of crazies fan out, eerily calm, and enter the abandoned supermarket.

INT. ABANDONED SUPERMARKET RUBBLE BUILDING, OUTLANDS - DAY

Roman climbs the barrier pile, stumbles, falls down to the other side. As he picks himself up off the floor he is stopped dead in his tracks by a sniper's rifle pointed right at him. But, is it the rifle or the beautiful WOMAN, 27, who holds the gun that freezes him?

The woman, too, for a fleeting moment, stares intriguingly at the sight of Roman. She's the first to snap out of it.

                    WOMAN
          Get out of the way.

Roman blinks back awake and steps aside. She steps atop a turned over shelf allowing her to easily see and aim over the barrier pile.

The sexy woman FIRES off three shots.

INT. ABANDONED SUPERMARKET RUBBLE BUILDING, FRONT, OUTLANDS - DAY

Two of Manus' group take kill shots to the chest, the third a gruesome kill shot in the head.

Manus and his group stop. Manus grunts his displeasure, his remaining group of crazies slowly back pedals away and out of the supermarket. Manus is pissed.

A fourth SHOT nets another head kill shot. Manus' group now runs away and to safety. Manus angrily retreats.

INT. ABANDONED SUPERMARKET RUBBLE BUILDING, SNIPER'S NEST, OUTLANDS - DAY

The woman now points her rifle at the still mesmerized and staring Roman. She steps down from her sniper's perch.

                    WOMAN
          Who are you?

                    ROMAN
          Someone in the wrong place at the wrong time.

                    WOMAN
          Aren't we all.

She lowers her weapon and kick slides a duffel bag to Roman's feet.

                    WOMAN (CONT'D)
          Can you shoot?

Roman unzips the bag and extracts two pistols. He begins to load the magazines.

                    ROMAN
          Who's that?

Roman head nods to the dead crazy on the floor nearby as big as Manus.

                    WOMAN
          A Dweller. Like the ones outside trying to kill you.
          Use to be their leader. Not anymore, obviously.

                    ROMAN
          He a friend of yours?

                    WOMAN
          Hardly. Was a business partner, well as much a
          business partner a Dweller can be. We had an
          understanding, which made an understanding with all
          of them out there too. Not anymore. Now, we just
          have...

Roman finishes loading his pistols.

                    ROMAN
          We just have what?

                    WOMAN
          Trouble.

As if on cue, a handful of Dwellers storm their position from the back like a stream of roaches crawling through the aisle rubble.

Roman's quick on the spot, surprising the woman, and FIRES FIRES FIRES! Dwellers are being picked apart by his shooting, but more continue to advance.

She's impressed by his skill and watches in awe as Roman successfully mows the Dwellers down.

Roman EMPTIES both clips and charges the last three! In the brutal hand to hand combat, Roman beats the last three down, rips the spiked spear from one of the Dwellers hands and finishes them off!

Roman turns to find the girl still impressively watching him then she snaps to, turns, hops on her sniper's nest and FIRES SUCCESSIVE SHOTS on the Dwellers advancing from the front!

Then all is quiet...

Roman drops his commandeered spiked spear, picks up the pistols, runs back to the duffel bag to find more bullets...there are none. He tries the other guns to only find they're all empty too.

                    ROMAN
          Out of ammo.

                    WOMAN
               (still aiming her rifle towards
                the front)
          It's been a long day.

The remaining Dwellers outside ERUPT in a LOUD WAR CRY!

EXT. ABANDONED SUPERMARKET RUBBLE BUILDING, OUTLANDS - DAY

The Dwellers retreat. Manus stands furiously in the parking lot in front of the store staring intensely inside...he slowly back steps away.

INT. ABANDONED SUPERMARKET RUBBLE BUILDING, SNIPER'S NEST, OUTLANDS - DAY

Roman hops up on the woman's sniper's perch, close to her. Her eyes dart to his presence.

> ROMAN
> What's happening? They're leaving?

> WOMAN
> They're regrouping.

She turns and they find themselves looking at one another...a moment shared...she doesn't like that and hops off the perch.

> WOMAN (CONT'D)
> We need to move.

> ROMAN
> Where?

> WOMAN
> The roof.

> ROMAN
> Let's just get out of here.

> WOMAN
> (walking away down the aisle)
> Can't. The Dwellers have us surrounded.

> ROMAN
> How do you know that?

> WOMAN
> How many times have you ventured into the OutLands?

She disappears around the corner. Roman hops off the perch.

> ROMAN
> (to himself)
> Apparently not as much as you.

He runs to catch up to her.

INT. OLD VAN, SIDEON - DAY

The windshield is almost fully covered in dirt, how RILEY, 25, can see out is a mystery to us, but she manages fine. She races pass the scattered pedestrians.

EXT. CENTER TOWN, SIDEON - DAY

Riley's old van barrels away from Center Town, PAN to follow the old van driving towards the outer walls and we find...off to the side of the road, a GIANT PILE OF BURNING BOOKS under the watchful eyes of TWO GUARDIAN SOLDIERS.

EXT. OUTER GATES OF SIDEON - DAY

Riley eases the van to the outer walls that surround Sideon, stops at the gates.

A giant sign: LEAVING THE CITY-STATE OF SIDEON. CONTINUE AT YOUR OWN RISK

A Guardian approaches.

                    GUARDIAN #1

     Riley.

She hands over a tin box. He looks around to make sure no one is watching, peeks inside the box and is satisfied.

                    GUARDIAN #1 (CONT'D)
     Be careful out there.

He steps back and lifts the iron bar. The van races on towards the horizon.

INT. OLD VAN, BORDERLANDS - DAY

Riley takes the desolate road leading further out into the nothingness. After a few stragglers carrying their sacks and bags, the road and terrain opens up to emptiness.

Riley tenses up upon seeing the Checkpoint and two Guardian soldiers up ahead.

                    RILEY

     Got a development.

She slides her pistol from her lap to the center console, covers it with a dirty rag. RENEE, 21, leans into view from the crate covered cargo in the back.

                    RENEE
     Shit. Guardians. What are they doing there? Road's
     suppose to be open and clear at this hour.

                         RILEY
          Guess we got bad intelligence.

Renee quickly checks the boxes, wicker baskets and container cargo in the back seatless
van. She scampers up to the front.

EXT. GUARDIAN CHECKPOINT, BORDERLANDS - DAY

DEVER, 28, tosses his smoke to the ground, KNOCK BANGS his rifle against the
Guardian pick up truck to wake up the tanning, napping FERELL, 22, laying on the
tailgate. In the bed of the truck is a METAL CAGE--the traveling jail cell.

                         FERELL
          What!?!

                         DEVER
          Got a bogey comin'. Look alive.

                         FERELL
          Don't know why you talked me into this new transfer.

                         DEVER
          I know what I'm doing. Police Mayor Syron's our
          ticket to a better life.

                         FERELL
               (getting up)
          If you say so.

Ferell jumps down, joins Dever in the middle of the road. Dever hands Ferell his rifle
and finger taps his pistol in its holster.

INT. OLD VAN, GUARDIAN CHECKPOINT, BORDERLANDS - DAY

Renee LOCK AND LOADS her pistol, stashes it between her seat and the center console.

                         RILEY
          Stay relaxed. Be smooth.

                         RENEE
          You people down here sure do see a lot of action.

                         RILEY
          If we go, we go on my move. Got it?

Renee gives her a playful look. Riley smirks.

                         RILEY (CONT'D)
          Do I need to remind you about Memphis?

                    RENEE
          (smiling)
     That *was fun.*

                    RILEY
     But, reckless.

                    RENEE
     Yeah, so you tell me. It was my first time.
          (a beat)
     And it's not called Memphis anymore.

                    RILEY
     It is to me.

Renee grins. Riley stops the van.

                    RILEY (CONT'D)
     Here we go.

EXT./INT. GUARDIAN CHECKPOINT/OLD VAN, BORDERLANDS - DAY

Dever approaches Riley, Ferell approaches Renee.

                    DEVER
     SHUT OFF THE VAN!

Riley does.

                    RENEE
     How we playing this, slut or scared?

Riley studies the two Guardians walking up.

                    RILEY
     Submissive and mute.

Riley manually rolls down her window. What a beauty! Dever definitely likes what he
sees.

                    RILEY (CONT'D)
     You two are new.

                    DEVER
     Transfers. Stamped out our share of moonshiners,
     Police Mayor Syron like what we do, brought us
     here.

                         RILEY
        Moonshiners?

                         DEVER
        Smugglers. Black Market runners.
                (steps closer)
        You two aren't transporting illegal goods, are you?

                         RILEY
        You think two little ole girls like us would be caught
        up in that stuff?

                         DEVER
        What ya have in the van?

                         RILEY
        Corn, flour, some tomatoes and apples, a few black
        beans. Normal stuff like that.

                         DEVER
        Let's see your papers and ID.

Riley hands over her ID paper and others. Dever reads the information on her ID. Flips
through the papers.

                         DEVER (CONT'D)
        The Barter Exchange. Sideon sanctioned. Seems all
        on the up and up. Where's her ID?

                         RILEY
        She hasn't had time yet.

Dever raises an eyebrow at her.

                         DEVER
        Why that's a violation.

                         RILEY
        The laws change so much nowadays it's hard to keep
        up. Especially when you spend all your daylight
        working to get food.

                         DEVER
        These laws are made for your benefit, that's why
        Police Mayor Syron deems them important.

                         RILEY
        Good way to keep everyone in line.

Dever LAUGHS...too hard. Riley plays along, smiles. He hands the ID and papers back to her.

Ferell, the pervert, stares at Renee. She just sits there, looking straight ahead. Ferell licks his lips.

                    FERELL
          What's ur name pretty girl?

Renee slowly turns her head and looks at him...just looks...

                    RILEY
          That's Renee. I'm Riley.

                    DEVER
          Nice to meet you Riley. Ferell, go check the cargo.

Ferell can't figure out this staring, non talking girl.

                    DEVER (CONT'D)
          Ferell!

Ferell snaps out of it, steps back, nods his head at Renee, CHUCKLING...points at her, then makes his way to the back of the van. Gets inside.

                    DEVER (CONT'D)
          Let's see the authorized City-State gas containers.
          Can't have you buying illegal black market gas now
          can we?

Riley reaches back and picks up the official Sideon issued gas can and gas paper card. Dever takes the paper card...hands it back. He takes the gas, shakes the half full container, opens it and takes a hearty smell.

                    DEVER (CONT'D)
               (smirking)
          Gas is the easiest product to counterfeit.

                    RILEY
               (trying to be playful)
          If you can find it.

                    DEVER
          Buy Sideon controlled gas once, then you can just
          keep filling it up with the illegal shit.

                    RILEY
          Are you ridiculing the policy on gas?

Dever, guard up now, LAUGHS at that, grins. He hands the container out to her--moves it away as Riley goes to grab it. He's enjoying this, hands it out to her again. She gives him a look...goes for it--Dever moves it out of her reach again. CHUCKLES. They stare each other down...

                    DEVER
          How we looking Ferell?

Ferell haphazardly checks the cargo inside the back. Picks up some corn, spills some beans, digs his hands into a basket of rice. He keeps stealing looks at Renee.

                    FERELL
          Seems all right.

                    DEVER
          You girls looking for any fun tonight?

Dever hands Riley her City-State issued gas can back.

                    DEVER (CONT'D)
          We know a place where we can taste a little booze.

                    FERELL
          Dever's right. Good, quiet place. Smoke a little
          grass, too.

                    RILEY
          Well, that's entrapment, Guardian. Why would you
          want to get me in trouble?

Dever studies her...grins...

Ferell reaches in deep into the flour basket...

                    DEVER
          You intrigue me, Riley. Do I intrigue you?

Riley puts on her best smile.

                    RILEY
          If I didn't have a schedule to keep...maybe.

Dever stares at her...intensity growing...Renee covertly slips her hand between the seat and console, grips her pistol...

In the back of the van, Ferell pulls out a wrapped closed bag, unties it.

                    FERELL
          We got contraband!

Dever, still relaxed.

                    DEVER
          What is it?

Ferell has another bag out. Renee moves her feet in closer, puts pressure on her toes.

                    FERELL
          Some sort of coffee I never seen before. Whole shit
          load of...
                    (tastes it)
          Sugar!

                    DEVER
          Now, Riley. Are you moonshining?

                    RILEY
          We just stumbled upon it. It's not that big of deal.
                    (silence from Dever)
          Would you like the sugar and coffee?

                    DEVER
                    (still playful)
          Are you trying to bribe a member of the regime?

Renee is getting nervous.

                    FERELL (O.S.)
          Oh shit!

                    DEVER
          What is it, Ferell?

Dever gets serious, ready, tries to look in the back. Ferell pulls out a HANDGUN from
the corn basket!

                    FERELL
          Weapons!

And just like that--Renee, lightning quick as a cougar, leaps into the back, DOUBLE
KICKS the surprised Ferell in the chest, sending him SPRAWLING OUT THE BACK
OF THE VAN!

Riley WHIP OPENS her door, CRASHING Dever to the ground while STARTING the
van!

Both Dever and Ferell tumble on the road as the van SCREECHES OFF! Dever
scrambles to his feet, his pistol out, FIRES! Takes aim...FIRES again as the van swerves

around Dever's pick up truck. The bullet STRIKES the TIRE, it POPS, SMOKES, Riley loses control, the van SLIDES off the road, CRASHES hard into the ditch and FLIPS on its side!

EXT. ROAD, CRASH SITE, BORDERLANDS -- DAY

We come up on the van, Riley and Renee, battered, crawl out the window of Renee's door and are met by the guns of Dever and Ferell.

                    DEVER
          Not a smart move.

                    FERELL
          You stupid bitches!

Ferell quick steps to Renee, JAM HITS the butt of his rifle into her gut, doubling her over. Riley flinches to move, but is stopped dead in her tracks by Dever's pistol being pressed to her head.

                    DEVER
          Don't move a muscle.

Ferell feels better, now having let that off his chest.

                    FERELL
          You don't hit a Guardian! Ever!

Renee straightens up with an evil grin directed at Ferell. Quickness again! Renee's GRAND SLAM KICK TO HIS BALLS forces Ferell over, he PUKES, drops to a knee. Renee steps back smiling her ass off.

Riley can't help but let a grin escape across her face. Dever, beyond angered, contains his composure and steadies his gun to Riley's head.

Ferell, however, has turned completely mad. He wobbly stands, spit frothing and raining from his mouth.

                    FERELL (CONT'D)
          You worthless whore!

WHAP! He cold clocks Renee with his RIFLE ACROSS HER FACE! Renee hits the ground.

Riley can't believe it! She has to help, Dever anticipates this move, shoves her to the ground. She looks up at Dever, tries to get up. Dever smiles.

                    DEVER
          Oh, honey. Stay down.

He raises his boot, SLAMS it to her head. Riley crumbles further to the ground like jelly, Dever on her back with his handcuffs out as...

Ferell DRAGS the almost knocked out Renee around the van, away from the prying eyes of Dever, Riley and us. We can only see RENEE'S LEGS sticking out. FERELL'S FISTS every once a while appear above the front of the van as he REPEATEDLY BEATS THE EVER LIVING SHIT OUT OF HER.

ON RILEY barely conscious, tears streaming, hands cuffed behind her back, still laying on the road with Dever straddling her back. She tries to get up to no avail.

                    RILEY
          RENEE!!! NOOOOO!

EXT. GUARDIAN CHECKPOINT, BORDERLANDS - LATER

CLANG! The metal cage door is SLAMMED SHUT. Dever LOCKS it. Riley, imprisoned in the makeshift jail in the bed of Dever's truck, sit crashes against the back, mesmerized, dazed, hurt, a shell. Dever STARTS the truck, takes off. We watch Riley go.

EXT. ROAD, BORDERLANDS - DAY

LONG ESTABLISHING SHOT of the crash site and lonely road. To the side of the scene, we make out a FIGURE HANGING from a makeshift pole.

                    KYRA (V.O.)
          How do you restrict the public in order to save the
          collective? How do you limit and take away
          freedoms without a fight?

EXT. ROAD, BORDERLANDS - DAY

We travel down the road, pass Riley's van still on its side in the ditch...

                    KYRA (V.O.)
          With so much power at stake, the rulers had to figure
          a way to propagandize out their iron clad rule in their
          City-States. They did this by instituting the Police
          Mayor System to control their regions.

...We come upon Renee hanging from the pole, beaten and dead.

                    KYRA (V.O.) (CONT'D)
          Old Timers saw this as nothing more than sugar
          coating the term Warlord.

A cardboard sign draped around her neck reads: SMUGGLER

                    KYRA (V.O.) (CONT'D)
          Call it whatever you want, crackdown violence and
          swift justice was a necessity for a Police Mayor to
          maintain his power.

EXT. ROAD TRAIL, ELITE SUBURBS, SIDEON -- DAY

ON Police Mayor Syron as he rides his Red motorcycle up the trail...

                    KYRA (V.O.)
          General Augustus Syron, Police Mayor for the City-
          State of Sideon, rose to power with his vicious Purge
          Campaign in the early years. Many welcomed and
          embraced Syron and his political arm, the 2nd Front
          Party. He and his Guardians eradicated the many
          evils, murderers, and inhumane individuals running
          wild.

EXT. POLICE MAYOR SYRON'S OUTER GATE, SIDEON - CONTINUOUS

TWO SENTRY GUARDIANS armed, uniformed, step aside to allow the Boss passage.
2nd Front Party flags wave atop the poles.

                    KYRA (V.O.)
          But, looking back, it was just a major power grab to
          take over control. Many see Syron as the worst of
          the Warlord Police Mayors.

EXT. POLICE MAYOR SYRON'S POND, SIDEON - DAY

Syron rides up to the waiting Dykes, hops off letting the bike go. Dykes is quick to catch
his Boss's bike before it hits the ground.

                    POLICE MAYOR SYRON
          What's the latest?

                    DYKES
          Junior took a team to the OutLands to find Ray.

EXT. ABANDONED SUPERMARKET RUBBLE BUILDING, ROOF, OUTLANDS -
DAY

The woman checks her ammo status, only three bullets left for the rifle.

                    WOMAN
          Shit.

                    ROMAN
          They're coming back!

Roman is maneuvering the hole infested roof seeing the horde of Dwellers emerge from
the rubble and brush surrounding the abandoned supermarket.

                    ROMAN (CONT'D)
          Any ideas?

                    WOMAN
          Just need to hold them off a little longer.
          Reinforcements are coming.

                    ROMAN
          How do you know that!?!

                    WOMAN
          Because I was suppose to be back in Sideon last
          night.

                    ROMAN
          Did you say Sideon?

                    WOMAN
          Yes. You know it?

                    ROMAN
          No, but that's where I was heading.

                    WOMAN
          Then stick with me and I'll get you there.

                    ROMAN
          Yeah, I can tell.

                    WOMAN
          You hear that?

Roman doesn't.

                    WOMAN (CONT'D)
          Look!

Roman looks to see the horde of Dwellers stop their advance then the SOUNDS of
motorized vehicles break through loudly!

                    WOMAN (CONT'D)
          They're here!

A group of Guardian trucks and jeeps break into the scene accompanied with the RAT-TAT-TAT-TAT of GUNFIRE!

The Dwellers scramble away, some getting clipped down before they can escape. Roman and the woman stand on the roof's edge watching blood bath.

Horace jumps out of a Guardian jeep.

                    HORACE
          RAY!?! RAY??

RAY, the woman, waves her arms.

                    RAY
          UP HERE!

Horace waves back.

                    ROMAN
          You're name's-

                    RAY
               (she leers at him)
          Don't start.

He grins at her, she doesn't like that one bit, looks away, a wall of ice now between them.

                    ROMAN
          Why is the big one just standing there?

Roman points to Manus as a Guardian truck stops before the massive Dweller leader. Junior hops out.

                    RAY
          What are you doing, Junior?

She intensely watches as Junior and Manus are in a heated discussion...

                    RAY (CONT'D)
          What are you promising?

Junior allows Manus to leave unharmed and he runs off into the brush.

Ray turns to find Roman is gone.

EXT. ABANDONED SUPERMARKET RUBBLE BUILDING, FRONT, OUTLANDS - DAY

Ray exits the supermarket to find Junior leaning against the Guardian truck with a shit eating grin on his face. She eyes Junior.

                    RAY
          Junior.

                    JUNIOR
               (emphasizing her "boy" name)
          Ray.

He spreads his arms out.

                    JUNIOR (CONT'D)
          Your big brother saving your ass yet again.

He LAUGHS that snarky laugh of his. What an asshole.

                    GUARDIAN #2 (O.S.)
          Found this one trying to escape out the back.

Ray and Junior turn to find two Guardian soldiers "escorting" Roman to the parking lot, a third Guardian behind him with a gun to his head. Roman is bleeding profusely from the side of his head.

Junior hops out of his leaning mode in pure excitement.

                    JUNIOR
          Holy shit, it's the Hunter! Horace look at this!

                    HORACE
          Well, ain't that somethin'.

                    JUNIOR
          Well, well, well, Hunter. Force him to his knees!

The Guardians obey, slamming Roman to the ground to his knees. Junior extracts his pistol.

                    JUNIOR (CONT'D)
          Been waiting all day to do this.

He walks right up to him and presses the barrel onto Roman's forehead. The anger and fury is unmistakable in Junior's eyes and face. He's going to kill him.

                    RAY (O.S.)
          Wait.

Like a child scorned, Junior huffs, turns to his sister.

                              JUNIOR

        Whaaattt???

                              RAY

        We need to interrogate him. He claims he was on his
        way to Sideon. We need to know why.

Junior spins looking to the sky in clear frustration. Ray simply shrugs at Roman when he
looks at her. The Ice Queen.

Junior's fury reaches its breaking point, turns back on Roman, gun pressed to his
forehead...

                              KYRA (V.O.)

        When the power went out during the third year of the
        war, the Old Timers, my grandfather's generation,
        said that changed everything. Information became
        the most sought after commodity on the planet.

...Junior relaxes slightly.

                              JUNIOR

        Take him to my compound. Squeeze every bit of
        information out of this hunter before you kill him.

                              KYRA (V.O.)

        It still is.

WHACK! Junior whacks the shit out of Roman with his gun knocking him unconscious.

EXT. POLICE MAYOR SYRON'S POND, TABLED AREA, SIDEON - EVENING

CONSTANCE, 22, is busy finishing preparing the table. Her beauty and sexiness is
amplified by the maid uniform she barely wears. We feel very turned on until we reveal
her face: lifeless, submissive, she's broken, a slave. Police Mayor Syron smacks her ass.
We feel sick in our stomach.

                        POLICE MAYOR SYRON

        You're rising my appetite, Constance!

Eyes on her work, she can't bear to look at him. Syron sits. Constance quickly finishes
setting the table.

                        POLICE MAYOR SYRON (CONT'D)

        What would I do without my lovely Constance?

EXT. POLICE MAYOR SYRON'S OUTER GATE, SIDEON - EVENING

The two sentries step aside on either side of the road as Junior in a Guardian truck races through.

EXT. POLICE MAYOR SYRON'S POND, TABLED AREA, SIDEON - EVENING

THREE TEENAGERS awkwardly stand before the seated Police Mayor not knowing what to expect.

>   POLICE MAYOR SYRON
>   You three are my leaders. My MVPs.

He places a box on the table, nods for them to take it. The tallest boy grabs the present.

>   POLICE MAYOR SYRON (CONT'D)
>   And there's more where that came from.

>   THREE TEENAGERS
>   (in unison)
>   Yes, sir. Thank you, sir.

Syron is proud, the boys frightened. Syron smile fades, back to business.

>   POLICE MAYOR SYRON
>   You have shown exemplary service in the 2nd Front's
>   youth watch program. I am entrusting you to show
>   and pave the way for the younger ones. We have a
>   lot at stake here boys, pride for our City-State being
>   the most important. Remember you represent the
>   people of Sideon and you represent me. I know you
>   will not fail me.
>   (holds his look on them...)
>   Eyes and ears always open. Keep up the good work,
>   boys.

With a wave, the boys leave and Constance sets down his juicy big ass deer steak. Least the Police Mayor eats good. She pours the wine from the decanter into his glass. Junior approaches the table.

>   POLICE MAYOR SYRON (CONT'D)
>   You're late.

>   JUNIOR
>   Ray's back.

>   POLICE MAYOR SYRON
>   I know.

                    JUNIOR
        The Dwellers have changed leaders, *again*.
                (Syron looks up from his meal)
        It's taken care of.

                POLICE MAYOR SYRON

    Ha!

Syron goes back to his meal.

                POLICE MAYOR SYRON (CONT'D)
                (mumbling to himself)
        Should just wipe out the whole lot of 'em anyway.

                    JUNIOR
        Uh, there's been a development with smugglers at the
        southern BorderLands checkpoint.

Police Mayor Syron pushes his plate away.

                POLICE MAYOR SYRON
        You've ruined my meal. We have a potential volatile
        situation with Miramar. If I can't control the
        smuggler problem in my own City-State it'd be the
        opening they'd take advantage of to ruin me.
                (SLAMS his hand on the table)
        This make me look weak! Enemies are continually
        trying to ruin *my kingdom*! And this is what you
        came in here with?
                (I can't believe it smiles)
        Two smugglers. One dead. One captured. The new
        guys, Dever and Ferrel.
                (chuckling now)
        This is what you bring to me? During my steak !?!
        Unbelievable. Yeah, I heard. I know *everything* that
        happens in my State.

                    JUNIOR
        Told Dever to stand down until I talked to you.

                POLICE MAYOR SYRON
        You goddamn right you did!

                    JUNIOR
        I'm on top of this situation...Let me be.

                    POLICE MAYOR SYRON
                  (sarcastically)
          You sure it won't interrupt your barbaric fighting
          entertainment?

Syron leans back, brain in overdrive, not listening.

                    JUNIOR
          Its not entertainment, its an investment.

Syron stops this talk with a wave of his hand.

                    JUNIOR (CONT'D)
          Look, I know this could be an explosive situation for
          us if not handled properly.

Syron bolts back to the table, SLAMS his fist, startling Junior.

                    POLICE MAYOR SYRON
          No, you are wrong. This is our opportunity!

He brings his steak back.

                    POLICE MAYOR SYRON (CONT'D)
          Listen to me now. Find out precisely what this
          smuggler woman knows, use it and we break the ring
          wide open.

                    JUNIOR
          Who said anything about a ring? These are just some
          insignificant small time girls.

                    POLICE MAYOR SYRON
          Nothing in the moonshiner's world is insignificant.
          Even if its just a slight peephole through that curtain.

                    JUNIOR
          What do I do with Dever and Ferell?

                    POLICE MAYOR SYRON
          I don't give a shit about Ferell. Dever, however, is a
          very capable soldier. He his your weapon. Do what
          you have to. Violence is a powerful tool.

                    JUNIOR
          Yes, sir.

Syron eyes him.

POLICE MAYOR SYRON

You're lucky that you're my only son. Otherwise...
    (lets it hang)
Solve this smuggling ring problem. We lose control
and we lose everything. I want the Black Market
shut down for good.

JUNIOR

Yes, sir. I caught the Hunter, too. He was holed up
with Ray. She says he was on his way here to
Sideon.

POLICE MAYOR SYRON

Interesting. Work your magic on him, too. Find out
who he is, where he came from. I want to know
everything.

JUNIOR

Yes, sir.
    (walks off)

POLICE MAYOR SYRON

And my ride...?

JUNIOR

    (turns around)
The Suburban is being fixed as we speak. Be ready
by the morning.

POLICE MAYOR SYRON

Tell the Hunter thanks for my deer steaks.

A shot at Junior and they both know it. Those steaks were suppose to be Junior's.

POLICE MAYOR SYRON (CONT'D)

Last thing.

Junior's at full attention.

POLICE MAYOR SYRON (CONT'D)

Get your house in order. Won't say it again.
Constance!
    (she reappears)
Bring my meal to my study.

She nods as Syron gets up and leaves.

EXT. ROAD TO BARTER EXCHANGE, SIDEON - MORNING

BILL, 50s, rides his bicycle along the road, a small cargo box strapped to the back. He passes the foot traffic walking to and from the Exchange with their own cargo.

The barbwire fence that encompasses the Barter Exchange land area doesn't allow for traders or proprietors to enter the grounds except through the outer gate.

EXT. OUTER GATE, BARTER EXCHANGE, SIDEON - MORNING

Bill rides up to the Guardian soldiers lounging on their two Guardian pick up trucks. He must pass them to gain access to the dirt road that leads to the Barter Exchange.

A soldier checks through his crate quickly then waves him through.

EXT. DIRT ROAD, BARTER EXCHANGE, SIDEON - MORNING

Bill rides in further into the wooded land away from the road and outer gate.

EXT. BARTER EXCHANGE, SIDEON - MORNING

The tin walled encampment of the Barter Exchange comes into view. Bill rides through more foot traffic and passes the Preacherman already on his box prophesying to the masses, who still pay him no mind.

Bill parks his bicycle by the entrance/exit section where more Guardians wait. The final checkpoint for entering and exiting the Exchange. Bill stands in line.

EXT. BARTER EXCHANGE, ENTRANCE/EXIT, SIDEON - MORNING

Guardian soldiers pick through and inspect the traders' baskets of corn, rice, apples, and etc. Bill waits in line behind TWO PRETTY GIRLS. The Guardians take their sweet ass time to gawk and flirt more at the two ladies than to inspect their goods.

> GUARDIAN #2
> Oh, no, here comes Ray.

They all turn to look.

> GUARDIAN #3
> Shit.

> GIRL #1
> Who's that?

> GUARDIAN #3
> A ruthless hard ass, that's who.

                    GUARDIAN #2
                 (scolding Guardian #3)
            And one of our bosses. Remember that.

                        BILL
            She's a beauty, though.

                    GUARDIAN #2
            Avoid Ray like the plague, old timer. Got one hell of
            a mean streak.

The bad ass, don't fuck with woman everyone calls Ray walks by the entrance with her
BEVY of GUARDIANS. She is the femme fatale, sexy, hot, and she's fucking deadly.

EXT. BARTER EXCHANGE, TIN WALL FENCE, SIDEON - MORNING

Ray's Guardians stop as she continues on to Syron and Junior.

                    POLICE MAYOR SYRON
            There's my lovely daughter.

                        RAY
            Father.

They hug briefly.

                    RAY (CONT'D)
            Junior.

                        JUNIOR
            Ray.

                    POLICE MAYOR SYRON
                 (to Junior)
            Don't you have some interrogating to do at the
            Compound? Walk.

And that's the end of it. Syron turns back to his daughter, ignores the sulking Junior
storming off. Syron EXHALES.

                    POLICE MAYOR SYRON (CONT'D)
            Oh, that brother of yours. If he wasn't my own blood
            and flesh I'd...

                        RAY
                 (yeah, right!)
            Mmmm, mmuh.

> POLICE MAYOR SYRON
> What's the word?

> RAY
> I've got business to attend to.
> (rolls her eyes)
> With those damn Corsican Brothers.

> POLICE MAYOR SYRON
> They're good pets to have.

> RAY
> Easy for you to say.

Syron hops in his Red Suburban.

> POLICE MAYOR SYRON
> Let Junior do his thing with our prisoners then you go
> in there and clean up after, find the information we
> need about this smuggler ring.

> RAY
> No doubt.

> POLICE MAYOR SYRON
> (laughs)
> That's my girl.

EXT. BARTER EXCHANGE, ENTRANCE/EXIT, SIDEON - MORNING

The Guardians at the entrance/exit finally allow the girls to enter with their goods. They quickly search Bill's box, allow him entry.

EXT. BARTER EXCHANGE, INNER GROUNDS, SIDEON - MORNING

Bill weaves his way through the open air arena of the Exchange, through the various "booths" containing a unique array of everything from tomatoes to vehicle and generator parts to handmade clothes. A truly low rent yard sale type survival arena.

Bill passes the center where crudely built billboards list the 2ND FRONT'S RULES AND REGULATIONS on bartering. Atop the billboards are the 2nd Front Party's flags and the picture of Police Mayor Syron, reminding you of Hitler and the Nazi regime...the 'always 2nd Front Party's Big Brother watching over you' propaganda tool.

EXT. BARTER EXCHANGE, THE CORSICAN BROTHERS' BOOTH, SIDEON - MORNING

The CORSICAN BROTHERS, MARKUS, 30, and DEUCE, 25. They deal in just about everything, can build or repair anything. Motorcycle, tractor, lawn mower, generator parts and tools scatter the place. Markus is currently working on a small motorcycle, parts everywhere. Deuce finishes stacking the vegetable crates. He's all covered in black soot.

> DEUCE CORSICAN
> Payment in full.
> (looks at Markus' progress)
> Hey, Dipshit! He expects his bike to be ready by today!

> MARKUS CORSICAN
> It will be.

> DEUCE CORSICAN
> Doesn't look like it. We got paid and usually when you pay for services you *expect* the service to be done! Yet here's the old man's bike *still* in a million goddamn pieces!

> MARKUS CORSICAN
> Easy for someone who just grabs boxes to bitch from the sidelines.

> DEUCE CORSICAN
> I just finished making fifty bullets! Real work.

> MARKUS CORSICAN
> Freakin' B team. I'm doing *real* work here! So pipe the hell down!

> DEUCE CORSICAN
> Move aside, Chump Change!

Deuce swipes the wrench from Markus. Markus stands, faces off against Deuce.

> MARKUS CORSICAN
> And what do you know about gear boxes!?!
> (swipes the wrench back)
> Now, be the woman you are and clean this shit hole up or sweep or something. Let the real men work!

                    DEUCE CORSICAN
                  (swipes the wrench back)
              Screw you and step aside.

Bill walks up, stands next to OLIVIA, 23, holding a cardboard box. They both look at
the comical display of Deuce and Markus "fighting" over the wrench.

                       OLIVIA
              Seems the Corsican Brothers are at their usual
              selves...like always.

                        BILL
              Guess we come back later when they cool down?

                       OLIVIA
                  (smiles)
              They never cool down.
                  (to the Corsicans)
              Hey assholes!

Both look menacingly at the voice, then both relax.

                   OLIVIA (CONT'D)
              Let Markus finish the bike and come work on my
              generator.

Deuce sarcastically bows his obedience, walks over with a look on his face.

                   OLIVIA (CONT'D)
              Don't give me your smart ass look.

                    DEUCE CORSICAN
              What's in the box, Olivia?

                       OLIVIA
              Well, it's not soap. Parts, you idiot.

Markus has to pipe in from under the motorcycle.

                   MARKUS CORSICAN
              You two are nothing but noise pollution. Either get it
              on or do me, Bill here and this whole damn region a
              favor and avoid each other like the plague.

Markus gets back to work, Deuce turns around to Markus.

DEUCE CORSICAN

Get it on!?! No one asked you to pipe in, numb nuts!
(turning back, mumbling)
Like I would anyway.

MARKUS CORSICAN

Ha! Like any of us believe that crap!

OLIVIA

He couldn't have me anyway, Markus.
(looks to Deuce)
No matter how much he wants it.

DEUCE CORSICAN

You're the one pursuing me, girl. *And I'm* the one
saying...
(for effect)
No chance!

That's it! Markus stands back up.

OLIVIA

As if you have a say in the matter.

Before Deuce can continue this game of theirs--

MARKUS CORSICAN

That's it! Enough. Everyone knows, including Bill,
that Deuce's in to you.

They all look at Bill, he smiles and nods his agreement.

OLIVIA

See, shit for brains!?! Even Bill sees right through
you. You can't have me.

DEUCE CORSICAN

(to Bill)
I'm being falsely accused, sir. Trust me on this.

MARKUS CORSICAN

Careful, Deuce's a shyster piece of shit! Give him some

> (cups his mouth for
> exaggerated conspiracy
> effect)

Illegal drink and you'll hear him profess his undying attraction for this girl. The more he drinks, the more he cries about her.

DEUCE CORSICAN

That's complete bullshit! I never cry. Plus, you can't count anything I say when I'm drunk.

OLIVIA

Ha! I knew it! See, I told ya.

MARKUS CORSICAN

Hold on there generator whore.

OLIVIA

> (playfully mouths the words to
> Deuce)

Generator whore?

MARKUS CORSICAN

You got no room to talk with your usual box of generator parts. Either you're running a side operation on generators...

OLIVIA

Am not!

MARKUS CORSICAN

Or you have a damn generator possessed by the devil himself cuz apparently it breaks every Goddamn time after I fix it.

DEUCE CORSICAN

We...

> (off Markus' look)

Every time after *we* fix it.

MARKUS CORSICAN

Whatever.

                    OLIVIA
        Can't help it if you two jokers are the only so called
        mechanics in town.

Olivia and Deuce stare at each other, neither of them giving in to the other...Markus goes
to Bill.

                MARKUS CORSICAN
        See what I mean.

Bill looks at them, smiles, then back to Markus.

                    BILL
        I do. How's the progress?

They both look at the motorcycle Markus has been working on.

                MARKUS CORSICAN
        By tomorrow. You messed it up real good. You
        been jumping the creeks again, haven't you?

                    BILL
            (grins)
        Trying to relive my youth I guess.

                MARKUS CORSICAN
        Nothing wrong with that!
            (looks at Bill's box)
        What's that?

                    BILL
        I have acquired a large sum of charcoal
            (presents the box)
        and its no secret that you two are quite adept with
        making bullets.
            (looks at the dirty Deuce)
        Apparently you do all the grinding of the charcoal.

                DEUCE CORSICAN
        The grinding, the casing shells, the igniting caps, et
        cetera.
            (to Markus for effect)
        All of it.

                MARKUS CORSICAN
        So, you want to barter the charcoal for what? Or do
        you need the bullets?

                              OLIVIA
          Oh, no, here comes Ray.

They all turn to look.

                         MARKUS CORSICAN
          Shit.

                          DEUCE CORSICAN
                    (a bit nervous)
          It's all good, I got her order ready.

                              OLIVIA
          What kind of name is Ray anyway?

                               BILL
          Police Mayor Syron called her Ray cause he wanted
          another boy.

                          DEUCE CORSICAN
          She's quite a sight though, ain't she?

                              OLIVIA
          Ass.

                          DEUCE CORSICAN
          What? She is.
                    (Olivia leaves)
          Damn it.

                               BILL
          Not smart, son.

                          DEUCE CORSICAN
          I know.

                         MARKUS CORSICAN
          Get her order ready.

Deuce goes to the back, grabs the four tin ammo boxes full of new, usable bullets.

                    MARKUS CORSICAN (CONT'D)
          Best you come back later.

                               BILL
          You're right about that.

Bill leaves with his charcoal just as Ray arrives at the neighbor's booth. The Guardians stand their distance. No one here is that stupid or that suicidal to mess with Ray.

EXT. BARTER EXCHANGE, NEIGHBOR'S BOOTH, SIDEON - MORNING

The sight of Ray sends the PROPRIETOR into a state of panic.

> RAY
> You have my payment?

> PROPRIETOR
> Al-al-almost.

> RAY
> Two days, asshole. You had two days.

> PROPRIETOR
> Ye-yes, ma'am. I know.

He scrambles, comes back with a large, towel covered crate. Ray peeks inside.

> RAY
> That's not the correct allotment we agreed on.

> PROPRIETOR
> I-I-I'm trying.

> RAY
> You think I give a shit about *your trying*? Either do
> or be done.

She gives a SHARP WHISTLE.

> PROPRIETOR
> (begging)
> No. Please.

Ray will have none of that. Impressively, she slashes out, grabs the man by the collar, hurls him over his booth's table to the ground and WHALLOP KICKS him hard in the ribs. The Proprietor WAILS in pain.

The Guardians get there destruction on! With that done, she heads straight to the Corsicans.

EXT. BARTER EXCHANGE, THE CORSICAN BROTHERS' BOOTH, SIDEON - CONTINUOUS

Deuce, holding the ammo boxes, gulps. Markus cautiously stands there wiping his hands with a rag.

                           RAY
              Markus. Deuce.

Deuce just nods his hello.

                      MARKUS CORSICAN
              Ray.

                           RAY
                   (to Deuce)
              You look that way cause of me?

                      DEUCE CORSICAN
              Yep.

He hands over the tin ammo boxes. She opens each one. Order's good. She's satisfied.

                           RAY
              Good work. See you next week.

Ray leaves, the Guardians stop thrashing the neighbor's booth and follow her out of the
Exchange.

Whew! A sigh of relief from both Markus and Deuce.

                      MARKUS CORSICAN
              Go see if he's okay.

Markus returns to work on Bill's motorcycle. Deuce walks over to check on their
neighbor picking himself up off the ground.

EXT. BARTER EXCHANGE, ENTRANCE/EXIT, SIDEON - MORNING

As Ray exits the Exchange a Guardian walk rolls her motorcycle right up to her.

                           RAY
              Got business to attend to at Junior's Compound.
              You're in charge here until I get back.

                      GUARDIAN #4
              Yes, ma'am.

Ray KICKS IT TO LIFE, TAKES OFF.

EXT. JUNIOR'S COMPOUND, SIDEON - DAY

Establishing shot of the compound as the sun wakes from its morning slumber. High
fences bathed with razor wire surround the premises. Its a junkyard with a warehouse
sitting in the middle.

EXT. JUNIOR'S COMPOUND, ENTRANCE, SIDEON - DAY

We follow the riding Ray as she enters into the compound, 2nd Front flags and emblems about, memories of the old Nazi regime enter your thoughts. The Guardians at the razor wired gate and throughout the compound let her pass through without another thought.

EXT. JUNIOR'S COMPOUND, JUNKYARD, SIDEON - DAY

A rustic warehouse houses itself in the middle of the property, surrounded by junked vehicles throughout.

EXT. JUNIOR'S COMPOUND, ROW OF JUNKED VEHICLES SIDEON - DAY

Two Guardians escort Roman down the row of junked vehicles, Junior, happy as can be, follows behind.

> JUNIOR
> Oh, you're gonna get it now, Hunter! Whoo! This is
> gonna be fun! Strap 'em to Betty!

The Guardians lead Roman to Betty, a carcass of an old large tractor with pipes and metal mash sticking out every which way.

Down the aisle at the far end is Ray berating three Guardians. She looks down over at Junior's fun. Ray catches Roman being pushed hard to Betty. She watches...

Roman is slammed hard face first against the tractor, arms forced up and tied off to a jutting out pole. As the Guardians tie his hands Roman catches Ray staring at him.

They lock eyes...

Junior twirls his whip. WHACK! Roman buckles, Ray looks away and gets back to berating her Guardians.

Junior WHACKS the whip again against the back of Roman's knees!

> JUNIOR (CONT'D)
> Who were those deer for, Hunter? Huh? Gonna sell
> them on the Black Market?

> ROMAN
> Was going to eat them.

Junior LAUGHS, drops his whip.

> JUNIOR
> You lie!

A punch to Roman's ribs! Junior gets close to Roman.

                    JUNIOR (CONT'D)
          I can do this all day.

He turns back to his two Guardians.

                    JUNIOR (CONT'D)
          Let's rack him! I hadn't racked anybody in three
          months!
                    (no response)
          Don't stand there with your thumb up your asses! Go
          get the four wheelers. Now!

The two Guardians run off.

                    JUNIOR (CONT'D)
          AND THICK ROPE! DON'T FORGET THE
          ROPES!

Junior, CHUCKLING, turns his attention back to Roman.

                    JUNIOR (CONT'D)
          You think after your limbs get ripped from their
          sockets you'll tell me what I need to know? Huh,
          tough guy!?! Whoo!

He PUNCHES Roman in the ribs again.

                    RAY (O.S.)
          Junior.

Ray's walking up.

                    JUNIOR
          Oh, great, the party assassin. You really care what I
          do to this sack of shit?

Ray glances at Roman, they lock eyes again, she looks back to her brother.

                    RAY
          Not in the slightest. But, he's not going anywhere,
          unlike you. Your *employees* have arrived for your
          event tomorrow.

Junior stares at her...realization then hits.

                    JUNIOR
          Shit, my whores are here!?! You coming to the fight
          tomorrow? Gonna be one hell of a show!

                    RAY
        Better get going. You don't want one of your boys to
        test drive the girls before you do.

Junior smiles and CHUCKLES at her. He's a sick bastard and he loves it.

                    JUNIOR
        Will this ever end?
                (spreads his arms out)
        And the son shall inherit the Earth!

Junior happily storms off leaving Ray questioning herself on what he just meant.

Ray SHARP WHISTLES to her two Guardians down the row. The Guardians head her
way. She walks up to Roman.

                    ROMAN
        Thanks.

                    RAY
        Don't thank me yet.

Ray whips out her knife, cuts him loose. Roman one knees it to the ground, holds his
battered ribs.

                    RAY (CONT'D)
        What'd you do?

                    ROMAN
        Hunted deer.

                    RAY
        Ha! You are an idiot aren't you. Nothing I can do
        about that.
                (to her Guardians)
        Take the prisoner to the holding bay.

INT. JUNIOR'S COMPOUND, WAREHOUSE, HOLDING BAY - EVENING

The dingy, barren, tin walled room with the stained concrete floor is not a place that
radiates comfort. Chains hang from the walls, the concrete floor funnels all water, fluids,
and blood to the drain in the center. A high placed broken small window allows the
setting sun's rays to barely light the space.

The two Guardians force Roman to the back corner away from the door, crudely chain
lock his ankle that attaches to the wall.

They leave. The heavy metal door SLAM CLOSES and LOCKS.

Roman gets to a sitting position, curls his legs and knees up close, drops his head, resting them on his arms.

The heavy metal door UNLOCKS, SWINGS out and opens. Ray enters with a chair, sits on it in the middle of the room. She waits for him to look up...he finally does.

                    RAY
          Up on the roof you told me you were headed here to
          Sideon. Why?

                    ROMAN
          Why not. What's it matter to you?

                    RAY
          Curious. You've had training. I noticed you could
          handle yourself quite well against the Dwellers. Are
          you a soldier?

                    ROMAN
          You noticed me, huh? Noticed I could fight.

She EXHALES, not enjoying his answers or his attempts at flirting. Ice Queen.

                    RAY
          Stop with the antics and answer my question. Are
          you a soldier?

                    ROMAN
          Ex. What's it matter?

                    RAY
          It matters on why an ex soldier would come to
          Sideon. What are you running from? Where are you
          from? Are you here to disrupt our peaceful City-
          State? Are you an advance soldier from a distant
          City-State sent here to scout our defenses. Yeah.
          Unanswered shit like that. It matters.

Roman's turn to EXHALE in this conversation.

                    ROMAN
I'm from back East. Where? Doesn't fucking matter.
There so many warring City-States now I don't even
remember. I've fought in so many wars and on so
many sides it's hard to keep up. Am I running from
something? You bet your ass I am. I'm done. I've
had enough bloodshed and death for two lifetimes.
All I want now is for it to be quiet. And as for your
utopia *peaceful* Sideon?? Ha!
          (leans up)
This place is nothing more than fear and intimidation.
You try to hold on and squeeze so much power that
you don't even realize how bad your precious rule is
cracking. I've heard of Sideon, we all have, heard of
the iron fisted rule of Syron-

                    RAY
And you want me to believe you chose this place to
receive your *quiet*?

                    ROMAN
Beats being at constant war or in one of the chaotic
City-States.

Roman leans back against the tin wall, looks away from her. She stares at him, anger
boiling...

                    RAY
Nice speech. To bad I think it's all complete bullshit.

Roman is stoic, still won't look her way...

                    RAY (CONT'D)
          (gives up)
I've done all I can.

She gets up with her chair and gets to the metal door. She turns back one last time.

                    RAY (CONT'D)
You're on your own now, Hunter.

She CLANGS the metal door SHUT and LOCKS it.

Roman leans his head against the tin wall, closes his eyes, takes another DEEP BREATH
and EXHALES...

The metal door UNLOCKS and SWINGS OPEN.

                                    DEVER
                         (entering)
                    You got yourself a new roommate, Hunter.

Roman opens his eyes to see Riley being shoved into the room. Riley eats concrete and
Dever is right on top of her chaining her ankle then attaching the chain to the hook on the
wall like Roman's.

                               DEVER (CONT'D)
                    You two love birds have fun.
                         (laughs)
                    Hunter, you better start talking or you won't be
                    staying with us long.
                         (to Riley)
                    You can learn a lot from him on what not to do
                    during your stay here. You cooperate, you will be
                    treated fairly, you act like that fool then your last few
                    days will be hell.

Dever looks down at her, thoughts flying through that brain of his...he glances at Roman
on the floor across the room, back down to the helpless Riley. Dever UNZIPS his fly.

This immediately prompts Roman up off the floor to charge at Dever! The chain
TIGHTENS just short of Dever. Dever laughs at him. Roman wants to beat the shit out
of Dever, but his chain won't allow it.

Riley looks at Roman for the first time, a slight spark of life ignites in her since her
ordeal and Renee's death. She lifts up off the ground to get a better look at this guy
trying to defend her honor.

Dever keeps taunting Roman, dancing around, darting in and out from him. Roman
simply stands over the drain in the middle of the room, his eyes the only part of his body
moving as he follows Dever's every move. Roman would kill this bastard if only he
could get the chance.

                               DEVER (CONT'D)
                    Look at the fury in you, Hunter. Bet you'd love a
                    shot at me.

                                    ROMAN
                    Take these chains off and let's see.

Dever LAUGHS at that. Stops. Looks hard at him.

                                    DEVER
                    In due time. In due time.

Dever walks over to Riley.

                         DEVER (CONT'D)
              Our dance ain't done yet either, firecracker.

Riley takes a swing at his legs but misses wildly. He LAUGHS at her then leaves the
room CLANGING the metal door SHUT and LOCKING it.

Roman looks at Riley on the floor. She doesn't know what to expect from him. Will he
be like Dever and Ferell? But, she gets her answer as he slightly nods, grins to her then
goes back to his corner and sits.

Riley lifts herself up and plants her back against her tin wall, sitting now facing Roman
across the holding room. Roman feels her gaze, shifts and turns to face her.

                            RILEY
              You're bleeding.

Roman checks the slash marks in his pants behind his knees where Junior whipped him.
Blood has trickled out, most of it crusted. His shirt is also spot covered with red crusted
up blood.

                           ROMAN
                   (slight grin)
              Not the first time.
                   (a beat)
              What'd you do?

She stops staring at him, looks off.

                            RILEY
              Trafficking of illegal contraband. Attempted assault
              on a Guardian soldier, possession of firearms,
              etcetera etcetera.
                   (she looks back his way, hard)
              They murdered my friend. That one,
                   (points to the door)
              Dever, strung her up and hung her from a pole.

                           ROMAN
              I'm sorry.

She looks away.

                            RILEY
              Yeah, well.

                           ROMAN
              They killed my friend too.

Riley looks back at him, softens up. They been through the same shit.

                    RILEY
          What they get you for?

                    ROMAN
          Wrong place at the wrong time.

                    RILEY
               (looks away)
          Aren't we all.

Roman lifts his shirt up a bit, checks out his battered ribs, gently touches the now purple and red area.

                    RILEY (CONT'D)
          Dever do that to you?

                    ROMAN
          No. This is the work of the lovely psychotic named
          Junior. He's a real peach.

                    RILEY
          I've heard.

                    ROMAN
          Name's Roman.

                    RILEY
          Riley.

                    ROMAN
          Well, Riley, how bout we figure a way out of here.

She smiles at that.

                    RILEY
          Already ahead of you.

She reaches the back of her head, lifts up her hair, begins digging something out that's been hidden underneath.

EXT. JUNIOR'S COMPOUND, SIDEON - EVENING TO NIGHT

The sun goes to bed for the night...

EXT. ROAD TRAIL, ELITE SUBURBS, SIDEON - DAY

ON Police Mayor Syron's Sideon's FLAGS and the 2nd Front Party FLAGS twirling in the wind. We pull back to reveal the tiny flags on each side of the front hood of the post Apocalyptic fitted Black Hearse. This vehicle has no problem doing maneuvering on or off road.

EXT. ROAD TRAIL, POLICE MAYOR SYRON'S OUTER GATE, SIDEON - DAY

The Black Hearse flies through Syron's front gate.

EXT. POLICE MAYOR SYRON'S MANSION, FRONT, SIDEON - DAY

Constance opens the door for Syron. Dykes approaches.

> POLICE MAYOR SYRON
> Sit rep.

> DYKES
> Here's Ray's report on the prisoners at the
> Compound.

He hands over the typewriter written page. Syron quickly scans it.

> DYKES (CONT'D)
> And Junior's back in the OutLands securing our
> interests there. Apparently this new leader of the
> Dwellers, Manus, is very eager to do business with
> us.

> POLICE MAYOR SYRON
> Good. He just may have kept his sorry lot of people
> alive a little bit longer.

Syron heads to the door.

> DYKES
> Sir, there are some developments we need to discuss
> before the cabinet meeting. Pertaining to Miramar
> and our smuggler ring problem.

> POLICE MAYOR SYRON
> Good or bad?

> DYKES
> Excellent, sir.

This stops Syron.

POLICE MAYOR SYRON
Constance, bring us a couple of drinks to the study.

Constance bows her head in obedience, enters the mansion.

POLICE MAYOR SYRON (CONT'D)
Has the Cabinet arrived?

DYKES
They have sir. Enjoying refreshments in the
conference room as we speak.

POLICE MAYOR SYRON
Good. Let those insufferable bastards wait until
we've concluded this new business of yours. And our
guest of honor?

DYKES
Here and waiting as you requested.

They enter Syron's mansion.

INT. POLICE MAYOR SYRON'S SANCTUARY, SIDEON - DAY

Syron's study, his elite, luxurious man cave. Syron sits at his magnificent, Mafia Don
type desk.

Walls are lined with shelves upon shelves of books. Plush couch, two cozy side chairs,
magnificent glass table with elephant tusks as legs, mini bar, and soft music playing from
the record player plugged into his mini gas powered generator. A lap of luxury.

Constance sets down the wine decanter and two glasses on his desk. Syron quickly
finishes his drink, motions Constance to refill his glass. She does then steps off to the
side.

DYKES
Intelligence from our assets inside Miramar have
brought us some enlightening news that we can
exploit.

POLICE MAYOR SYRON
Dykes I swear to God I'll break your fucking neck in
two if you keep talking in platitudes and don't just
give it to me straight.

                              DYKES
            The Minister of Agriculture, one of our guys, gave
            me this official government document proving that
            Miramar is actively supporting and providing for the
            Black Market activities specifically in Sideon to
            undermine your rule.

Dykes hands over the typewriter written document for effect. Syron reads...smiles.

                          DYKES (CONT'D)
            They also have active agents currently running inside
            the smuggler ring based in Sideon. Read the names.

                      POLICE MAYOR SYRON
            We have a mole.

                              DYKES
            We have a mole.

                      POLICE MAYOR SYRON
            When does Junior return?

                              DYKES
            Later tonight or tomorrow morning.

Syron scribbles words on a piece of paper.

                      POLICE MAYOR SYRON

      DALLAS!!

He folds it, seals it inside a big envelope, puts it inside a folder. DALLAS, 12, runs
inside and to Syron.

                  POLICE MAYOR SYRON (CONT'D)
            Deliver this to Junior at the Compound during his
                      (making fun)
            spectacle tomorrow.

Dallas' eyes grow wide.

                             DALLAS
      Yes, sir!

The kid runs off.

                    POLICE MAYOR SYRON
          Let the word out about our detainee, let's see whose
          cage it rattles.
                    (more to himself)
          I'll need to rethink interrogation strategies with Ray
          too.

                    DYKES
          I have some ideas as well, sir.

                    POLICE MAYOR SYRON
          I'm sure you do, Dykes.

He slams back his wine, refills.

                    POLICE MAYOR SYRON (CONT'D)
          Smugglers and Miramar...I will bleed their world dry.

Syron stands, walks for the door.

                    POLICE MAYOR SYRON (CONT'D)
          Get to it then.

                    DYKES
          Yes, sir.

Dykes downs his wine.

                    POLICE MAYOR SYRON
          Constance, you will show him out.

Constance, back to them at the mini bar, transforms her beaten spirit and sad face into a
million dollar smile and sexpot aura. She turns around.

                    CONSTANCE
          Yes, sir.

Syron and Constance share a quick look before he leaves.

INT. POLICE MAYOR SYRON'S MANSION, HALLWAY, SIDEON - DAY

Syron continues down the pristine hallway to the double doors at the end. Horace
appears at his side.

                    POLICE MAYOR SYRON
          Bring him in.

                    HORACE
          Yes, sir.

INT. POLICE MAYOR SYRON'S MANSION, CONFERENCE ROOM, SIDEON -
DAY

The FIVE MEN, ranging from 40 to their late 50s, seated around the impressive brown
oak table turn their attention to the doors as they open.

TWO GUARDIAN SOLDIERS and Horace transport the black hooded prisoner to the
front of the room, force sit him down into the chair at the head of the table. Horace and
the soldiers step back off to the side.

>   POLICE MAYOR SYRON (O.S.)
>   The time has come for you gentlemen to choose your
>   path.

The five seated men turn their attention from the hooded prisoner to the Police Mayor at
the doors. Their looks immediately reconfirm to us that Syron is *the* force to be reckoned
with. His presence commands respect and fear. The five men cower lower in their
chairs. These men of power in this room are Syron's subjects and they know it. Syron
knows this as well.

>   POLICE MAYOR SYRON (CONT'D)
>   The time of our fractured regime is over.

Nobody is brave enough or stupid enough to speak or interrupt him. Syron slowly walks
towards the prisoner at the head of the massive table.

>   POLICE MAYOR SYRON (CONT'D)
>   You are all capable and impressive Ministers for the
>   government of Sideon. But, the time has come for us
>   all to be aligned, to solidify under the banner of the
>   2nd Front Party. To pledge your loyalties to me.
>   Your leader. Our new world demands it.

Syron whips off the prisoner's hood.

>   POLICE MAYOR SYRON (CONT'D)
>   Karl Melbourne, my very own Minister of the
>   Interior, how nice of you to join us.

MELBOURNE'S eyes Syron with pure hatred.

>   MINISTER MELBOURNE
>   (contempt)
>   Syron. What is the meaning of this?

POLICE MAYOR SYRON
(to the room)
It is time for you to choose your path.
(bends down closer so only
Melbourne can hear)
You think you could try and overthrow me without
me knowing of it? I know *everything* that happens in
my kingdom.

MINISTER MELBOURNE
(to the room)
He will trash you aside too! You'll be nothing more
than his sheep!
(to Syron)
You are not a King!

Syron eerily smiles, pulls out his emerald laden dagger.

MINISTER MELBOURNE (CONT'D)
You are not a GOD!

Syron nods and his two soldiers step forward and hold Melbourne down.

POLICE MAYOR SYRON
You have made your choice.

He effortlessly slides the dagger into Melbourne's side, oddly sensuous like.

POLICE MAYOR SYRON (CONT'D)
Now, should we start with the 2nd Front Party
Chairman?
(he points the dagger to the
Chairman)
Or, with my Minister of Labor?
(points to the Labor Minister)

MINISTER MELBOURNE
(struggling)
Go to Hell.

POLICE MAYOR SYRON
You are in Hell.

Syron walks over to the 2nd Front Party Chairman, places the dagger on the table before
him.

POLICE MAYOR SYRON (CONT'D)
Choose your side.

The Party Chairman slowly grabs the dagger, stands and walks over to Melbourne and stabs him easily into his gut. Then one Cabinet member after the other all take their turns and ease the dagger into Melbourne's body. Not death by a thousand cuts, but death by six slices. Syron's loyalty and regime solidified.

EXT. POLICE MAYOR SYRON'S MANSION, SIDEON - DAY

Melbourne is kicked out the front doors, bloodied, dying, rolls down to the driveway.

Syron, followed by his five Cabinet members, walk out. Horace hands his boss the crossbow. With all watching, Syron steps over to the dying Melbourne, aims his crossbow at his face.

Syron looks to the petrified Cabinet members.

> POLICE MAYOR SYRON
> You have pledged your loyalty and obedience to me
> and you shall receive riches and power beyond your
> comprehension. If you defy me...

Syron fires the Crossbow into Melbourne's face!

> SYRON
> Well...just don't. I have eyes everywhere.

EXT. THE CITY-STATE SIDEON - DAY TO EVENING

Shots of the walled off City-State...

EXT. BORDERLANDS - EVENING

...to shots of the lands, fields, and wooded area surrounding Sideon known as the BorderLands...

EXT. BORDERLANDS, FARMING FIELDS - EVENING

We see under the watchful eyes of Guardian soldiers the share cropper laborers finish their farming work for the day as the sun goes down and walk back to the safety of the walled off Sideon.

EXT. BORDERLANDS, WOODS - EVENING

We pass through the woods and the sparsely different clusters of various tent encampments where those that prefer to live out from under the rules and protection of Sideon live.

EXT. CORSICAN BROTHERS' CAMP, BORDERLANDS - NIGHT

We come upon the brothers' large wooden barn that reminds us of the time before the wars.

INT. CORISCAN BROTHERS' BARN, BORDERLANDS - NIGHT

Deuce is gently pouring out his bag of black gunpowder on the wooden table. Wicker baskets of charcoal sit besides the grinder next to the table.

Lanterns are strung about overhead providing more than ample light.

Olivia BURSTS inside the spacious barn startling Deuce.

                    DEUCE CORSICAN
          Damn it, girl! You can't do that. You're gonna get us
          both killed.

                    OLIVIA
     Huh?

                    DEUCE CORSICAN
               (spreads his arms out)
          Making explosives here.

She gently enters further taking everything in.

                    OLIVIA
          You're joking right? You can't do that. Make
          explosives.

                    DEUCE CORSICAN
          Sure you can. Take charcoal and potassium nitrate or
          saltpeter.

                    OLIVIA
               (rolls her eyes)
          Yeah, sure.
               (maybe he's not full of it)
          Explain.

                    DEUCE CORSICAN
          Saltpeter. The household name for potassium nitrate.
          You can make saltpeter, just takes manure, ashes,
          urine,-

                    OLIVIA
     Gross.

                    DEUCE CORSICAN
          -dirt, green plants, filters, some time, the sun, things
          like that.

She nods to the five constructed "hand grenade" containers on the table. Deuce smiles,
time to impress.

                    DEUCE CORSICAN (CONT'D)
          Homemade hand grenades. Take a clean, empty
          condensed-milk can or substitute, fill it with the gun
          powder or dynamite, if you have any, add small
          pieces of iron until your can is full, seal the top, leave
          a small hole for your fuse, craft and attach a small
          wooden handle at the bottom.

                    OLIVIA
          Doesn't explain how it explodes.

                    DEUCE CORSICAN
          The explosive reaction is based on the principle of a
          combustible material, charcoal, combined with an
          oxidizing agent, potassium nitrate or in this case
          saltpeter. Combining a material that burns easily
          with another which in the chemical reaction will
          supply the necessary oxygen for the combustible's
          consumption.

                    OLIVIA
          You sound like Markus.

                    DEUCE CORSICAN
          Ha. Only when talking explosives.

                    OLIVIA
          How do you know all this stuff?

                    DEUCE CORSICAN
          Markus. We have a lot of books, illegal ones, novels,
          textbooks, magazines. As a kid he divided the
          subjects up between us, he pointed me towards the
          chemistry and science materials.

                    OLIVIA
          And he learned how to build and fix things.

Olivia reaches the table, wants to touch the homemade hand grenades.

                    DEUCE CORSICAN
      Don't!
                    (he moves her back)
            This combination is highly sensitive and unstable.

She sees his hands still on her arms...she looks at him.

                         OLIVIA
      I'm impressed.

They lean towards one another...they are inches apart...the moment finally arriving...the
kiss...but-

                    MARKUS CORSICAN (O.S.)
            Jesus! Enough you two!

Markus enters, the two step away from each other, embarrassed and disappointed that the
kiss didn't happen.

                    MARKUS CORSICAN (CONT'D)
            The materials ready?

                    DEUCE CORSICAN
            Five grenades ready to go. When's the delivery
            scheduled?

                    MARKUS CORSICAN
            Change of plans. We're using them.

                    DEUCE CORSICAN
      On what?

                    MARKUS CORSICAN
            The tin walls holding Riley.

                         OLIVIA
      WHAT!?!

                    DEUCE CORSICAN
      Riley?

Markus whips out a typewritten sheet of paper.

                    MARKUS CORSICAN
            An official Guardian's report of the incident. This
            particular one was intercepted while on its way up
            north.

                    DEUCE CORSICAN
         Who'd you get that from?

                    MARKUS CORSICAN
         Don't worry about it, Loud Mouth.

Deuce rolls his eyes, takes it, reads the typewriter written paper report.

                    DEUCE CORSICAN
         Renee's been killed.

                    OLIVIA
         The new girl? This can't be!

Olivia snatches the report, quickly scans the paper.

                    OLIVIA (CONT'D)
         Riley's been taken!?!

                    DEUCE CORSICAN
         We can't let them get away with this.

                    MARKUS CORSICAN
         We won't. We're gonna bust her out.

Deuce looks up with new resolve.

                    DEUCE CORSICAN
         Revenge time.

                    MARKUS CORSICAN
         Not just about revenge, Deuce. We have to protect
         the network. Many names, many families could be in
         danger. The network, its people, that's *our*
         responsibility.

                    DEUCE CORSICAN
              (incredulous)
         You think Riley will break!?!

                    MARKUS CORSICAN
         Not yet. But everyone eventually does.

                    OLIVIA
         Wait! You can't be going off doing something
         stupid.

                    MARKUS CORSICAN
          I'm not gonna let her sit there-

                    DEUCE CORSICAN
          Me neither! And they killed Renee!

Olivia knows.

                    OLIVIA
          This is it, then. This is the beginning.

Markus gets it, understands. Deuce still confused.

                    MARKUS CORSICAN
          What she means is welcome to the opening theater in
          the new war of attrition.

                    DEUCE CORSICAN
                 (Jesus Christ!)
          Why do you have to talk like that sometimes? Just
          say revolution!

                    MARKUS CORSICAN
          Doesn't sound as cool.

Deuce rolls his eyes.

                    DEUCE CORSICAN
          How we doing this?

                    MARKUS CORSICAN
          Hit 'em fast, hit 'em loud, break her out, then prepare
          for war.

                    DEUCE CORSICAN
          Amen to that. Our own personal war.

                    OLIVIA
          What can I do?

                    MARKUS CORSICAN
          A detailed layout of Junior's Compound.

                    DEUCE CORSICAN
          How would she...!?!
                 (looks at Olivia)
          How would you know that?

                    MARKUS CORSICAN
          She use to work there.

                    DEUCE CORSICAN
               (shocked)
          What!?!

                    OLIVIA
          Waitress. Strictly as a waitress.

                    MARKUS CORSICAN
          Can you do it, Olivia?

                    OLIVIA
               (still looking at Deuce)
          I know the place.

                    MARKUS CORSICAN
          Olivia?

                    OLIVIA
               (to Markus)
          I can map the layout.

                    MARKUS CORSICAN
          Get the grenades ready, Deuce.
               (Deuce is still in shock)
          Deuce!

                    DEUCE CORSICAN
          Huh?
               (finally looks from Olivia to
                Markus)
          What?

                    MARKUS CORSICAN
          We leave at dawn.

                    DEUCE CORSICAN
          What does the old man say?

                    BILL (O.S.)
          The old man says no.

They turn to find Bill.

MARKUS CORSICAN

Two smugglers caught, one killed, the other jailed.
She's one of us! She's ours to protect!

BILL

There's a bigger picture here.

DEUCE CORSICAN

We run the Black Market! We are the smugglers'
leaders!

BILL

And I'm the Revolutionaries leader! You do this and
Syron will reign hell down on us.

OLIVIA

We have to fight one day.

They all look at her.

OLIVIA (CONT'D)

I mean, that's what you, we, all of us have been doing
these last years. Preparing, strategizing, gathering for
war. Might as well be now.

MARKUS CORSICAN

Prepare yourself Bill. Get the people ready. We're
breaking Riley out.

Bill EXHALES, closes his eyes and pinches his nose. He knows this is happening,
there's nothing he can do. It is what it is. He looks back to Markus and gives him a nod.

EXT. JUNIOR'S COMPOUND, SIDEON - DAY

Establishing shot Junior's Compound as the sun wakes from its sleep.

EXT. JUNIOR'S COMPOUND, ENTRANCE, SIDEON - DAY

We follow the running kid messenger, Dallas, as he enters into the compound, 2nd Front
flags and emblems are more heavily about, a Nazi-esque grand holiday for Junior's event.
The Guardians at the razor wired gate and throughout the compound know who Dallas is
allowing him free reign.

EXT. JUNIOR'S COMPOUND, JUNKYARD, SIDEON - DAY

The Kid messenger runs his way pass the rustic warehouse, all through the property
surrounded by junked vehicles.

EXT. JUNIOR'S COMPOUND, JUNKYARD, FIGHTING AREA, SIDEON - DAY

A cleared out area among the various junked cars, vans, and machines. Barbwire ropes off the arena, the fighter's ring. It's not a heavy crowd, but it is a RAUCOUS one. Hard core fighting is *the* sporting entertainment in this post Apocalyptic world.

2nd Front groupies and "off the clock" Guardians taunt, yell, and wave 2nd Front Party flags from on top of junked vehicles that line the entrance path to the "boxing ring", a truly intimidating entrance for the opposing fighter.

Dallas runs through it all carrying his thick brown folder.

EXT. JUNIOR'S COMPOUND, JUNKYARD, FIGHTING AREA, VIP SECTION, SIDEON - DAY

A roped off "VIP" section with lawn chairs, shade umbrellas and bikini clad women waitresses is the kid's destination. Sitting in the best spot wearing sunglasses is Junior. Horace off to his side.

Junior spots the messenger, sets down his tall glass boat drink of alcohol. Dallas holds out the folder.

                    JUNIOR
          Relax, kid. Not time for business yet. Sit.

At first unsure, the kid then sits on the ground before Junior still holding the folder now facing the ring.

Behind the ring, the GIANT CHALKBOARD ODDS BOARD is being tending to by an EMPLOYEE, who constantly chalks and erases the various changing odds and different bets coming in for the fight.

Dallas checks out the crowd...sees someone he knows. He almost acknowledges and waves at the person, but Markus slowly shakes his head no. The kid hasn't survived this long without being smart and knowing when to keep his mouth shut. The kid averts his eyes and they land back on the fighting ring.

BOOM, BOOM...BOOM, BOOM! WAR DRUMS. The BAND'S DRUMMERS furiously BEAT the large drums signaling the start of the event. The crowd CHEERS in anticipation.

Walking down the path towards the ring is a massive monster of a man, THE PRIDE, 29. He wears no robe, only tape on his fists, black and red shorts, black shoes and no socks. Junior leans down to Dallas.

                    JUNIOR (CONT'D)
          That's The Pride of Sideon, kid.

The kid looks up at the board and sees that The Pride is the huge favorite over some challenger named Rocks. Junior stands and APPLAUDS.

The crowd ERUPTS, cheering on their favorite fighter. The Pride steps between the barbwire, enters the ring.

A RING OF BOOS welcomes the second man walking the path to the ring, ROCKS, 23. A gigantic man in his own right.

                    JUNIOR (CONT'D)
          They call him Rocks. From Miramar. They say he
          smashes rocks with his fists to train. I think its
          complete bullshit.

EXT. JUNIOR'S COMPOUND, JUNKYARD, FIGHTING RING, SIDEON - DAY

The vicious fight begins to the absolute ENJOYMENT of the crowd. The two brawlers trade punches back and forth, standing toe to toe. You can tell it's going to be a great fight.

EXT. JUNIOR'S COMPOUND, JUNKYARD, FIGHTING AREA, VIP SECTION, SIDEON - DAY

The brutal first round comes to end with the crowd CHEERING. Junior is smiling. His fight and event are perfect.

                    JUNIOR
          Hand me the folder. This from the Boss?

The kid stands, hands over the folder. He's now sad because with the delivery done, he won't be able to watch the fight.

                    DALLAS
          Yes, sir.

                    JUNIOR
          You want to stay and see the fight?

                    DALLAS
          Yes, sir!

                    JUNIOR
          Ok then. Go sit over there.

Dallas runs off to the spot Junior pointed to. Junior opens the folder, rips open the envelope and reads the paper...

                    JUNIOR (CONT'D)
          Shit.

He tosses the folder to Horace.

                    JUNIOR (CONT'D)
          I'll be back in a minute.

Horace quickly scans the paper. He gets up to join Junior.

                    JUNIOR (CONT'D)
          No, sit back down. Stay here. Keep an eye on things
          while I take care
                    (points to the folder)
          of that.

EXT. JUNIOR'S COMPOUND, JUNKYARD, FIGHTING AREA, SIDEON - DAY

Junior walks towards the warehouse, passing the ring as the two fighters square off and begin round two.

We see Deuce in the crowd watching Junior the whole way walking from the ring arena. Deuce jumps off the junked car, slips away.

EXT. JUNIOR'S COMPOUND, JUNKYARD, ROW OF JUNKED CARS, SIDEON - DAY

Deuce walks directly to the brown El Camino parked between two junked vans. He carefully pulls back the tarp covered back to the crates holding his homemade hand grenades.

INT. JUNIOR'S COMPOUND, WAREHOUSE, HOLDING BAY, SIDEON - DAY

Riley furiously works the bobby pin into the ankle lock.

                    ROMAN
          Thought you said you were good at this.

She gives him a good nature shut the hell up look.

                    ROMAN (CONT'D)
                    (grinning)
          Maybe by next week-

The RATTLING of the locks on the metal door quickly stops her, she palms the bobby pin.

The door OPENS, Junior enters, his 9mm at his side and Dever trailing with a machete. Junior walks straight to Roman, gun extended, Roman stays still in his seated position.

                              JUNIOR
            On your knees.

Roman complies.

                         JUNIOR (CONT'D)
            Your last chance. Answer my questions or suffer
            before you die.

Dever walks up to Roman with the machete, twirls it in his hand with a creepy smile on
his face. Junior now goes to Riley.

                         JUNIOR (CONT'D)
            Interesting information on you. Interesting friends.

He squats down close to her.

                         JUNIOR (CONT'D)
            What am I going to do about that?

He looks her up and down...

                         JUNIOR (CONT'D)
            What to do...Guess we're gonna have to *pump* you
            free of that information that's in
                    (taps her head)
            that cute little head of yours.
                    (that psychotic grin of his)
            I'm gonna get first crack at you before someone else
            does.

Dever turns from Roman, smiles at Riley.

                         JUNIOR (CONT'D)
            Answer our questions and you won't have to worry
            about Dever or the Compound full of angry men out
            there touching you. Me, however, I just
                    (he touches her hair)
            might have to touch you regardless.

Junior lets his eyes fall down to her breasts, keeps them and his focus there. Riley's
chance! Lightning quick, she bolts up on him, kicking her leg up, wrapping the chain
around the now shocked Junior's neck and falls back to the concrete. Impressive! She's
going to choke him to death.

Dever slashes down at Roman who moves away just in time, then rushes Riley! Just as
Dever is about to slam into Riley-

KABOOM! One side of the tin walled holding bay EXPLODES! Deuce's homemade hand grenade! All four crash to the concrete floor, dust fills the room making everyone blind.

                    MARKUS CORSICAN
          Riley!

                    DEUCE CORSICAN
          Anybody hurt?

The dust begins to clear...Markus has the bolt cutters out, CUTS the ankle chain on Riley.

Dever has a piece of tin sticking out of his chest. Dead. Junior lays motionless on the floor. Unknown.

Roman COUGHS, wobbly stands.

                    MARKUS CORSICAN
          Let's go!

Deuce is already through the hole he created. Markus guides Riley by the hand.

                    RILEY
          Wait!
               (they stop)
          Cut him loose too.

Markus looks at Roman.

                    RILEY (CONT'D)
          Do it!

But, instead, he tosses the bolt cutters to him, which Roman snatches out of the air. Riley and Markus are gone.

Just as Roman CUTS OFF his ankle chain, Junior wakes. Roman tries to scramble out the blasted hole. Junior FIRES!

                    JUNIOR
          Don't you move.

Roman turns around to see the kneeling Junior holding out his 9mm, struggling to get his bearings, his focus, and back to his feet.

Screw it! Roman charges Junior nailing him in a Ray Lewis football tackle hit! BAM! The gun FIRES then dislodges from Junior's hand and CLANKS onto the floor.

The bruising hit damages both men. They separate and reach their feet. For a split second they square off, staring each other down-bam!-They're at it again! A fight to the death that without a doubt is better than the one outside.

Both men each get the upper hand only to have the other one come back. They hurt each other and get hurt themselves. The fight is evenly matched and brutal.

EXT. JUNIOR'S COMPOUND, JUNKYARD, FIGHTING AREA, SIDEON - DAY

Pandemonium! The explosion has caused a mini panic. The fight has stopped, the Guardians have weapons drawn, the fans run aimlessly around for cover and the exit.

Deuce lobs another grenade into a group of junked pick up trucks-KABOOM! Chaos! Just what they need.

EXT. JUNIOR'S COMPOUND, JUNKYARD, ROW OF JUNKED CARS, SIDEON - DAY

Markus takes Riley to the El Camino, they get inside.

EXT. JUNIOR'S COMPOUND, EASTERN FENCE, SIDEON - DAY

Deuce tosses a third grenade against the fence-KABOOM! It tears an enormous hole through it.

INT. JUNIOR'S COMPOUND, WAREHOUSE, HOLDING BAY, SIDEON - DAY

The barbaric fight continues. Both men are going to kill each other. They slam into the exploded tin wall, separate, scramble away from each other.

Junior finds his 9mm in the rubble, runs to it, grabs it, turns to fire at Roman and WHOP! Roman kicks the gun from Junior's grasp, damaging his hand! Junior SCREAMS in pain!! Drops to his knees in agony!

Dever's machete! Roman gets it, stares Junior down, twirls the machete in his hand. Junior can't believe what is happening.

ROMAN
This is for Miller, you asshole!

But, before Roman can slice the machete into Junior, Horace comes barreling through the metal door, FIRES, misses! Roman throws the machete towards Horace, who easily dodges it, and has to scramble away leaving Junior alive.

Horace runs for a better angle to shoot and kill Roman with. Roman darts quickly, scoops up Junior's 9mm on the floor-FIRES! Horace ducks the shot, moves through the rubble, FIRES back!

Roman hops through the exploded tin wall hole, the bullet RICOCHETING off the dangerously close hanging tin, Roman RETURNS FIRE blindly BANG!-BANG!-BANG! sending Horace for cover as Roman escapes!

EXT. JUNIOR'S COMPOUND, JUNKYARD, SIDEON - DAY

Deuce runs to the speeding El Camino. Markus SKIDS to a stop, Riley opens the door allowing Deuce inside.

> DEUCE CORSICAN
>
> Eastern side!

Markus SPINS OUT and hauls ass!

EXT. JUNIOR'S COMPOUND JUNKYARD, FIGHTING AREA, SIDEON - DAY

Roman makes his way through the chaos, searches for a way out, anything...He runs on top of a junked van to get a bird's eye...Scanning, scanning, scanning...he spots the hole in the fence! Roman jumps off to race to it!

EXT. JUNIOR'S COMPOUND, EASTERN FENCE, SIDEON - DAY

Roman and the El Camino are converging on the same spot, racing from opposite sides. He waves for them to stop! They don't. The El Camino barrels on towards the hole.

Markus slows just enough to line up a straight shot for the car through the hole that allows Roman a chance to fly himself into the back bed.

The El Camino doesn't slow down enough and Roman can't catch up to make the attempted leap. The car SCRAPES through the hole. Roman runs for the hole as well.

INT. DYKES' DARK PICK UP TRUCK, SIDEON - DAY

Dykes eases his truck along the outer fence and just gets a view on the El Camino farther down. He slows even further.

The El Camino stops! Roman keeps running. Deuce leans out the window.

EXT. JUNIOR'S COMPOUND, EASTERN FENCE, SIDEON - DAY

> DEUCE CORSICAN
> HURRY UP IF YOU WANT A RIDE!

Roman leap flies into the back bed. Markus GUNS it!

INT. DYKES' DARK PICK UP TRUCK, SIDEON - DAY

Dykes smiles to himself as the El Camino makes its escape. He slowly follows its path.

INT. JUNIOR'S COMPOUND, WAREHOUSE, HOLDING BAY, SIDEON - DAY

Horace stands over the injured Junior.

> HORACE
> They escaped. Shit. This ain't good. What do we
> do?

Junior grabs the machete up off the floor, fury boiling through him, and lightning quick jams the blade inches from Horace's throat. Spit and saliva foam and drip from Junior's mouth.

> JUNIOR
> What do we do? What do we do!?!
> (he leans into Horace, the
> blade draws a trickle of
> blood)
> What do you do? You go bring them back and
> WHOEVER broke them out!! And where the fuck is
> Dykes!?!

Junior maniacally stares at Horace and his throat...he so badly wants to slice it open.

> HORACE
> (calmly)
> Someone needs to tell your father.

> JUNIOR
> Worry about the prisoners. Bring them back to me
> NOW!

EXT. WOODS, BORDERLANDS - DAY

The El Camino barrels through the woods, Markus knowing exactly where he's going. Roman holds on for dear life in the back bed. Markus slide stops the vehicle right next to a mess of a pile of trees, bushes, and branches.

Markus and Deuce jump out, Roman and Riley walk off to the side as the brothers reach into the foliage mess pile. They pull the coverage out, uncovering a Guardian pick up truck hidden beneath and out across towards the El Camino. The pile was a roped laden camouflaged cover! Deuce and Markus completely disappear the El Camino underneath the foliage cover.

> MARKUS CORSICAN
> (to Roman)
> Didn't know there'd be a fourth.

                    ROMAN
          You've done enough. Thank you.

                    RILEY
          He can help us.

                    MARKUS CORSICAN
               (sizing Roman up)
          No offense-
               (to Riley)
          -we don't know anything about him.

                    RILEY
          I know they don't like him.
               (smiles at Roman)
          And that he wants to kill Junior.

They all look to Roman, who simply shrugs.

                    ROMAN
          Unfinished business.

                    DEUCE CORSICAN
          What's your name, cowboy?

                    ROMAN
          Roman.

Riley grabs an extra shirt from inside the Guardian's truck.

                    RILEY
          Here.
               (tosses Roman the shirt)

                    DEUCE CORSICAN
               (a bit messing with him)
          You some kind of bad ass, Roman? Some soldier
          who's lost his way?

                    ROMAN
          Something like that. Although I haven't been a
          soldier for some time now.

Roman takes off his battered bloody shirt, uncovering his tortured bruised and cut torso.
His beating doesn't go unnoticed from the three. Then they notice Roman's symbol
emblem tattoo on his inside bicep near his arm pit. CLICK, CLICK!

Markus and Deuce have both their guns out, pointed at Roman.

                    MARKUS CORSICAN
          That's Syron's army tattoo!

Roman nods it's true.

                         ROMAN
          Not trying to hide it. I was branded in my youth,
          forced into fighting. Years ago, I escaped.

Roman puts on the shirt.

                    DEUCE CORSICAN
          To what?

                         ROMAN
          A new army, a different City-State, another war.
          Over and over again. Then I looked for something
          new.

                    MARKUS CORSICAN
          What?

                         ROMAN
          Peace. A place without killing and destruction. A
          simple life. But, you can't escape your fate. I tried.
          Just found more fighting and wars. I'm not running
          away anymore.

Deuce puts away his gun.

                    DEUCE CORSICAN
          And now you figure you need to kill Junior.

                         ROMAN
          He deserves to die. Among others.

                    MARKUS CORSICAN
          And then what? You kill Junior and what? You
          think that'll end it? Our suffering, our captivity?

                         ROMAN
          It's a start. Sometimes you have to fight for peace.

                    MARKUS CORSICAN
          Deuce?

                    DEUCE CORSICAN
          I believe him.

                    MARKUS CORSICAN
          Well, I don't.

But, Marcus does put away his gun.

                    MARKUS CORSICAN (CONT'D)
          We're heading south. You can hitch a ride with us
          for few miles but then you're on your own.

                    RILEY
          No. I'm taking him to Bill.

                    ROMAN
          I'm an ally. You're going to have to trust me on that.

                    MARKUS CORSICAN
          I don't even trust him.
                    (pointing to Deuce)
          So you're way down low on the trust factor.

                    ROMAN
          Remember I don't know who you are all as well.

                    MARKUS CORSICAN
          We're the ones that just broke you out of jail.

                    ROMAN
          That's why I'm giving you the benefit of the doubt.
                    (a beat)
          Right now.

Before this gets into a pissing contest or worst--

                    RILEY
          We can use him.

                    MARKUS CORSICAN
          And if we can't? If he's not who he says he is?

                    RILEY
          Then Bill will decide what do with him.

Markus holds his gaze at Riley...

                    MARKUS CORSICAN
        Shit.
                (a beat)
        Deuce grab the cuffs.
                (to Roman)
        You have a problem with that?

                    ROMAN
        Fair enough.

EXT. REVOLUTIONARIES ENCAMPMENT, BORDERLANDS - DAY

Hidden in the wooded hills of the BorderLands is the temporary Revolutionaries' camp.
Markus parks the Guardian pick up truck and they get out, but don't advance any further.
Roman hops out the back bed, still hand cuffed.

FOUR REVOLUTIONARY FIGHTERS emerge from the foliage completely invisible to
us just moments ago.

Running from the closest army tent up to Deuce is Olivia.

                    OLIVIA
        Where the hell have you've been!?!

She hugs Deuce, lets go. Goes to Riley.

                    OLIVIA (CONT'D)
        I'm sorry about Renee. Good to have you back at
        least.

The girls embrace. Olivia sees Roman.

                    OLIVIA (CONT'D)
        Who is this?

                    BILL (O.S.)
        Roman?

Bill walks out from the army tent.

                    ROMAN
        Hey Bill.

Markus, Deuce and Riley stand there confused.

Now more of the people in the many tents of the camp emerge to see what's going on.
Bill embraces Roman.

                         BILL
            Deuce, unlock those cuffs.

                        ROMAN
            Good to see you again, Bill. Been a long time.

Deuce unlocks the cuffs, eyes his brother. What the hell I going on?

                         BILL
            You got my message. I never thought Miller would
            find you.

                        ROMAN
            It was smart to send him. Only he could have found
            me.

                         BILL
            Figure you had a right to know, she being your only
            family and all.

                        ROMAN
            I got your message about two weeks ago. Got
            sidetracked when we were hunting deer to trade.
            Miller didn't make it.

That hurts Bill.

                         BILL
            He fill you in on our situation here?

                        ROMAN
            He did. Intriguing things you have going on here.
            Also about Constance. Is she still alive?

                         BILL
            Yes.

                        ROMAN
            She still there?

                         BILL
            She won't leave. She's positioned herself in a prime
            spot to gain very valuable information. Has it in her
            head that it's her duty to remain regardless how
            insanely dangerous it is.

                        ROMAN
            Sounds like her.

Deuce and Markus are still shocked and confused. They converse to themselves while still watching Roman catch up with Bill and talking to Olivia and Riley.

> DEUCE CORSICAN
> Well, this is surely interesting.

> MARKUS CORSICAN
> I don't like it.

> DEUCE CORSICAN
> You don't like anything.

> MARKUS CORSICAN
> Something's off here. With all of it. Stay alert.

> DEUCE CORSICAN
> Always.

INT. ARMY TENT, BORDERLANDS - LATER

Bill and Roman study the multiple hand drawn blueprints of Police Mayor Syron's mansion, interior and exterior. The Corsican brothers and Olivia stand off to the side.

> ROMAN
> I'm going there now. Give me some time to scout out
> the place before your war begins.

> BILL
> If I had anyone to spare I'd send them with you.

> ROMAN
> I know. You all have your hands full. I'll be fine.

Bill puts the drawings in the satchel, hands it to Roman.

> BILL
> New identification papers in there too.

> DEUCE CORSICAN
> Storming Syron's palace solo?..., that's dangerous.

> BILL
> He's right. Olivia take Roman to the weapons and
> gear tent. Take what you want.

> ROMAN
> Won't need much. See you on the other side.

Roman and Bill shake hands.

                    BILL

          Hopefully.

                    ROMAN

          Fellas.

The brothers nod, Roman and Olivia leave the tent. Bill can sense the brothers'
apprehension with the new developments.

                    BILL
          I've known him for a long time. Before you two.

                    MARKUS CORSICAN
          It's just...just that...

                    BILL
          Happening fast? Well, you wanted fast and so here it
          is.

                    DEUCE CORSICAN
          No getting out of it now.

                    MARKUS CORSICAN

          Nope.

                    DEUCE CORSICAN

          What now?

                    MARKUS CORSICAN
          Rally the troops. We make our stand at the Barter
          Exchange. We've planned for this. Time to put our
          defensive measures to test.

                    BILL
          Markus, I want you take a handful of guys and be
          ready to storm Syron's when the time comes.

                    MARKUS CORSICAN
               (smiling)
          Thought you said you had no one to spare.

                    BILL
          Yeah, well, how about that. Truth be told, Roman
          will be a great diversion. Take it out.

                    MARKUS CORSICAN
          Hopefully Syron will be there.

Deuce CHUCKLES.

                    MARKUS CORSICAN (CONT'D)
          What?

                    DEUCE CORSICAN
          Either way, once we take over the Exchange he's
          coming, they're all coming.

                    MARKUS CORSICAN
          Either way, it's going to end.

                    DEUCE CORSICAN
          Divide and conquer.

                    BILL
          We'll see.

EXT. POLICE MAYOR SYRON'S MANSION, FRONT, SIDEON - DAY

Syron is driven up the driveway in the Black hearse where Ray and Junior await by the
front of the mansion. They step out, Syron turns to his driver.

                    POLICE MAYOR SYRON
          Leave us.

The driver quickly scurries off. Syron has that rage boiling to the surface. He quick
steps up to Junior and WHALLOP PUNCHES him in the gut! Then he BACKHAND
SLAPS Ray across her face! His two children are stunned.

                    POLICE MAYOR SYRON (CONT'D)
          They escaped on both of your watch!

Dykes speeding dark pick up truck grabs their attention, Dykes pulls all the way up, gets
out.

                    DYKES
              (proudly)
          I followed them to their camp. I know the location of
          the rebels.

                    JUNIOR
          Lets send a brigade to wipe them out! Tonight!

                    POLICE MAYOR SYRON
          You would do that wouldn't you.

Junior's confused, Ray remains quiet and still. Syron is in deep thought, pacing a bit, he's quick to a plan.

                    POLICE MAYOR SYRON (CONT'D)
               (to Junior)
          How solid are we with this Manus character and the
          rest of 'em.

                    JUNIOR
          The Dwellers are back in our pocket. Manus comes
          cheaply.

                    POLICE MAYOR SYRON
          Give him whatever he wants. Dykes, you're to the
          Outlands, gather the Dwellers.

                    DYKES
               (not what he wanted to hear)
          Sir?

Syron doesn't hear Dykes weakly protest or care, he's in full on mode.

                    POLICE MAYOR SYRON
          Take the diplomat trucks and one armored personnel
          vehicle. Choose any of the new drivers and get your
          ass out there.

                    DYKES
          But...but...

Syron turns on him.

                    POLICE MAYOR SYRON
          You're a soldier goddamn it, act like it! You go get
          the Dwellers and invade that rebel camp! Leave no
          one alive, including the Dwellers. You understand?
          You think you can handle that?

                    DYKES
          Yes, sir.

                    POLICE MAYOR SYRON
          Go.

Dykes is off. Syron turns back to Junior and Ray.

POLICE MAYOR SYRON (CONT'D)
Put this place on high alert. Who knows what this
extermination will spawn. We must be prepared for
anything. Tell Horace to alert the Guardians and to
be on standby.

RAY
You knew there'd be an escape, didn't you?

Syron raises an eyebrow at his intelligent daughter. Junior's confused. But he remains
impassive on her question.

RAY (CONT'D)
Dykes. You orchestrated his tailing. You knew
they'd escape.

POLICE MAYOR SYRON
(now allows a nasty grin)
Knew they'd try. *Hoping* they'd succeed so I could
learn the location of the rebels' camp.

JUNIOR
(finally getting it)
Then why'd you hit us!?!

Syron laughs at this, shakes his head and storms off mumbling more to himself. Ray
answers the question for him.

RAY
Because they still escaped on our watch.

JUNIOR
Fuck him.
(spits)
What's your take on the crazies?

RAY
Involving the Dwellers? That is a bad move. An
overreaction. This could start a war.

JUNIOR
(to himself)
Maybe it's happening sooner than I thought.

RAY
What was that?

Junior turns to her.

JUNIOR

I wonder.

RAY

Wonder what?

JUNIOR

If we are starting a war, where you'll end up on the
side of things when it's all played out.

RAY

I'm not following.

JUNIOR

(smiles)
You never do.

He leaves her and heads right up to a Guardian. Ray sees him bark out orders and then
the Guardian runs off, hops on the motorcycle and takes off.

Ray watches Junior.

RAY

What's going on in that diseased brain of yours..?

EXT. THE CITY-STATE SIDEON - DAY

The motorcycle rider eases off the road by the outer walls of Sideon. Roman flips up the
visor of his helmet, takes out two pencil drawings from the satchel.

The drawing is a portrait of a man. Roman studies the drawing, then studies the full body
drawing of the same man.

He looks down the road to the South Gate of Sideon. In the near enough distance, there
are three Guardian soldiers. One bearded, one on the plump side and the third of what
could only be of the man in the drawings.

ROMAN

Hello, Boykins. Now, to walk the bike. I hope this
works as you said, Bill.

EXT. SOUTH GATE ENTRANCE, SIDEON - DAY

The three Guardian soldiers notice the man walking his motorcycle down the road
towards them. Boykins is quick to inspect.

BOYKINS

I'll take this one.

Boykins greets the rider, who promptly slips him a small wrapped box. Boykins takes the bribe.

                    BOYKINS (CONT'D)
          Papers.

Roman hands them over. Boykins pretends to thoroughly go over the identification papers, but his two fellow Guardians aren't even paying attention or care. Boykins waves Roman through, lifting the iron bar.

Roman KICKS the bike TO LIFE and drives inside Sideon.

EXT. BARTER EXCHANGE, SIDEON - EVENING

More people are milling about the front than usual. The scattered seven Guardian soldiers look bored and don't see any threat. The Preacherman is on his stage.

                    PREACHERMAN
          The Barter Exchange will be closing shortly. Please
          gather your belongings and disperse. The curfew is
          quickly approaching. You do not want to be caught
          outside in the night.

Like a broken record, the Preacherman repeats his statements. Deuce weaves his way through the crowd outside. He finds Bill.

                    DEUCE CORSICAN
          I count seven.

                    BILL
          We are ready.

                    DEUCE CORSICAN
          Olivia is inside.

                    BILL
          We'll wait for your signal.

They part ways.

EXT. POLICE MAYOR SYRON'S MANSION PROPERTY, SIDEON - EVENING

A pristine, manicured, palace spread that has withstood the hard times. If not for the Guardians, the outer razor wire and front military style checkpoint gate, one would think they traveled back in time before the days of the war.

EXT. OUTSKIRTS OF SYRON'S MANSION PROPERTY, TREES - EVENING

Roman lays in the brush and trees eyeing the Guardian activity at the estate with the binoculars. He rises and is on the move.

Roman runs parallel to the property then covertly advances closer.

EXT. POLICE MAYOR SYRON'S MANSION, BACK, SIDEON - EVENING

Roman's made his way to the back side of the property. He eats dirt just as a Guardian on an ATV MOTORS his way along the outer fence, completing his duty rounds. He rides out of sight.

EXT. BARTER EXCHANGE, ENTRANCE/EXIT, SIDEON - EVENING

Deuce walks up to the entrance/exit. He heads directly to a Guardian.

> GUARDIAN #2
> Deuce! Saw your girlfriend inside earlier. Oh, how I
> can't wait to love on that.

The three other Guardians nearby laugh along. Deuce smirks-then whap!-choke holds and turns around the Guardian stealing his pistol. Deuce holds the pistol out against the other three, with his Guardian as a shield.

> DEUCE CORSICAN
> Drop your weapons. Drop them or I kill him!

> GUARDIAN #2
> Shoot this asshole! That's an order!

BAM! A fired shot! A Guardian falls to his death behind Deuce, gun in his hands. Bill steps into view with his smoking pistol. He just saved Deuce's life.

The gunshot does two things: One, it startles and freezes the remaining Guardian soldiers outside. Two, it propels the people into action!

They bum rush the gates and the remaining Guardians with shovels, rakes, hammers, and whatever else they have. The action is swift and successful. A man runs onto stage and knocks out the Preacherman, takes his bullhorn.

> MAN
> THE PEOPLE ARE RISING UP! GUARDIANS
> THROW DOWN YOUR WEAPONS!

GUNFIRE erupts inside the tin wall fenced in Exchange. Deuce whacks his shield Guardian over the head, knocking him unconscious to the dirt.

                              DEUCE CORSICAN
       Olivia!

He rushes through the entrance/exit!

                              BILL
       Bring the chains!

Bill steps to the three Guardians kneeling with her hands behind their heads by their
unconscious mate.

                              BILL (CONT'D)
       We have ourselves some prisoners to keep.

EXT. ROAD TO BARTER EXCHANGE, SIDEON - EVENING

The lone road to the Barter Exchange is strangely quiet and without the usual foot traffic.

EXT. OUTER GATE, BARTER EXCHANGE, SIDEON - EVENING

The four Guardian soldiers are milling about the road and outer gate.

                              GUARDIAN #5
       No one else thinks this is strange? Where is
       everyone? Curfew is approaching.

DISTANT POPPING.

                              GUARDIAN #6
       Was that gunfire?

MORE DISTANT POPPING. The Guardian soldiers all look towards the Exchange but
can't see anything. They slowly go for their weapons.

Across the road behind them FOUR GRASS CAMOUFLAGED FIGURES rise up from
the tall grass field, all with rifles at that the ready.

                              RILEY
       HOLD IT RIGHT THERE. HANDS UP.

A warning SHOT is fired. All the Guardian soldiers immediately raise their hands.

                              RILEY (CONT'D)
       Turn around, slowly. Relieve them of their weapons.

A fellow Revolutionary does just that. Riley approaches the now grouped up Guardian
soldiers.

                    RILEY (CONT'D)
            Now. Take your clothes off.

But, then two Guardian pick up trucks appear on the horizon coming down the road to the
Exchange and outer gate.

                    RILEY (CONT'D)
            Shit.

Guardian #5 smiles at Riley.

                    GUARDIAN #5
            Shift change, you dumb bitch.

Riley WHACKS the Guardian across the face knocking him out and to the ground.

The two oncoming trucks pick up speed. Guardian #6 breaks free, runs desperately down
the road towards the pick up trucks waving his arms!

GUNFIRE ERUPTS from the oncoming trucks. The rebels FIRE BACK and take cover
behind the parked Guardian pick up.

Guardian #6 gets clipped in the cross fire.

Riley hops up into the back bed of the truck then UNLEASHES A VOLLEY OF SHOTS
at the lead truck! The windshield shatters, and the truck loses control and crashes off the
road, through the barbwire fence and into the field.

The second Guardian pick up truck STOPS, PEELS a 180 and HAULS ASS away.

                    RILEY
            Well, there went this plan. To the Exchange, boys!

EXT. BARTER EXCHANGE, INNER GROUNDS, SIDEON - EVENING

Panicked, Deuce runs through the melee. Some of the crowd is proceeding to knock
down the billboards in the center with all the 2nd Front's rules.

                    DEUCE CORSICAN
            Olivia!

He runs through more.

                    DEUCE CORSICAN (CONT'D)
            OLIVIA!!

He can't find her.

                    OLIVIA

          Deuce!

                    DEUCE CORSICAN

          Olivia?

                    OLIVIA

          Deuce!

She runs to him!

                    DEUCE CORSICAN
          You okay? What happened?

                    OLIVIA
          They opened fire on us. We fired back.

                    DEUCE CORSICAN

          Casualties?

                    OLIVIA
          Three of us, one of them.

He hugs her, relieved.

                    DEUCE CORSICAN
          When I heard...I thought...

She breaks away from him.

                    OLIVIA

          Hey dumbass!
               (smiles)
          You're not getting rid of me that easy.

He smiles, then plants a mighty kiss on her!...

                    BILL (O.S.)
          Okay. Enough. We got work to do.

They part as Bill walks up. Deuce smiling, can't take his eyes off of her, nor can Olivia take hers off of his...

                    DEUCE CORSICAN
          Bring everyone inside, close the gates, secure the
          fence and perimeter. We know what to do.

                    BILL
          That we do. We've been waiting a long time for this.

> DEUCE CORSICAN
> (turns to Bill)
>
> Wait.
> (Bill stops)
> Bring Dallas and his friends to my booth.
> (Bill leaves.)
> I've got a new wrinkle to try out.

> OLIVIA
>
> I bet you do.

EXT. POLICE MAYOR SYRON'S MANSION, BACK, SIDEON - NIGHT

The ROAR of the ATV approaches. Just as the Guardian rounds the corner, Roman dashes from the fence heading into the woods.

> ATV GUARDIAN
>
> HEY! STOP!

He GUNS it after him.

EXT. POLICE MAYOR SYRON'S MANSION PROPERTY, WOODS, SIDEON - NIGHT

Roman makes it into the first cut of trees, the ATV RAMPAGING ON, quickly catching up.

POV of ATV Guardian as Roman weaves through the trees then vanishes!

The ATV slow rolls further into the woods, the Guardian with his gun out.

The Guardian eases off his ATV, behind him we see Roman slither from out of sight stalking up to the Guardian.

Roman vice locks his arm and elbow around the unsuspecting Guardian's throat, cutting all his air off...silently. It's a struggle between the two, but Roman's a bit stronger and at a better tactical position...the Guardian drops quietly.

EXT. BARTER EXCHANGE, THE CORSICAN BROTHERS' BOOTH - NIGHT

Dallas and his GROUP OF FRIENDS ranging from Dallas' age, 12, to 21 gather around Deuce.

> DEUCE CORSICAN
> The first assault will be a ground one. To prepare for
> this, I'm charging all of you with our first line of
> defense. Land mines.

He steps aside to reveal on the tables bricks, nails, and shotgun shells. A giant pile of shovels lay on the dirt.

                    DEUCE CORSICAN (CONT'D)
          We don't have much time so pay attention. You have
          a lot of work to do.

                    DALLAS
          And this is going to stop them?

                    DEUCE CORSICAN
          Just need to slow them down. First you dig holes, as
          many as you can, around the Exchange.
                    (picks up a brick)
          You place the brick in the hole, pack your dirt firmly
          around it. Next, you place the nail
                    (grabs a nail)
          on the brick, pointed side up like so. Now watch.

He picks up a shovel, quickly digs a small hole. He puts the brick in the hole, firmly packs dirt around it, then places the nail. Firmly packs the dirt around that to stabilize the nail.

                    DEUCE CORSICAN (CONT'D)
          This is the tricky part so you must be careful. Take
          your homemade shotgun shell and place the blasting
          cap just on top of the nail.

He places the shotgun shell in the hole, just before touching the pointed side of the nail.

                    DEUCE CORSICAN (CONT'D)
          Pack your dirt firmly to stabilize your mine.

He packs the dirt around the contraption with the end side of the shell just an half an inch above ground.

                    DEUCE CORSICAN (CONT'D)
          Pack your dirt firmly. Then cover the shotgun shell
          with loose dirt.

Deuce covers the land mine, spreads the loose dirt around and over the land mine.

                    DEUCE CORSICAN (CONT'D)
          Hopefully, one of the invaders will unknowingly step
          on the shell, forcing the blasting cap onto the nail and
          BOOM! One soldier down with a mangled foot.
          Any questions?
                    (no response)
          Remember safety is your first priority. Get to it!

EXT. POLICE MAYOR SYRON'S MANSION, BACK, SIDEON - NIGHT

The three Guardian soldiers at the back gate stand at attention when the LIGHT of the
ATV headlight shines brightly right at them.

                    GUARDIAN #7
                    (stepping out)
          What is this?

The Guardian can't see the driver of the ATV because of the bright light.

                    ROMAN
          Perimeter secured.

The Guardian lowers his pistol as do the two behind him.

                    GUARDIAN #7
          This is getting to be such routine it's boring.
                    (turns around)

Roman leaps off the ATV and onto Guardian #7's back, immediately commandeering the
soldier's gun! The ATV rolls onward and bangs into the back fence by the other two
Guardians.

                    ROMAN
          Throw down your weapons! Now! Or he dies!

Roman steps towards them showing them their buddy in a choke hold with a pistol to his
head.

WHACK! Roman knocks out his Guardian with a wallop to the head with the pistol then
directly aims it at the two standing Guardians.

Before the soldiers figure out what to do, Roman skillfully flash attacks them,
SLAMMING the butt of the pistol onto the skulls of both Guardian soldiers. All three
down. He takes their weapons.

INT. BARTER EXCHANGE, INNER GROUNDS, SIDEON - NIGHT

Deuce is stretching out a thin hard wire across the yard, very low to the ground. A few others walk along the wire, pointing it out to the others.

Deuce reaches Olivia, who finishes planting the spike with the sledgehammer. Deuce ties off the wire, tests its tautness. Bill approaches.

                    BILL
          The escape route is prepared, concealed.

                    DEUCE CORSICAN
          Is it too much of a risk to bet on?

                    BILL
          No. And I believe its our only option. Our best
          option.

                    OLIVIA
          What is?

                    DEUCE CORSICAN
          Using their overconfidence against them. They'll
          believe they can quickly and easily take us out by a
          frontal assault. Won't attack from multiple sides.

                    BILL
          Strength in numbers. Won't want to spread
          themselves out too thin. One attack, one army, one
          side. Bulldoze us over.

                    OLIVIA
          I think you're right.
                    (grins)
          What match is a bunch of peasants with no weapons
          against them?

                    DEUCE CORSICAN
          Any word from our scouts?

                    BILL
          None yet.

                    DEUCE CORSICAN
          How's Dallas and his crew doing?

                         BILL
              (grins)
          Better than I expected.

                    DEUCE CORSICAN
          Good. Cocktails, weapons, ammo, grenade-

                         BILL
          It's going good, Deuce. We're prepared. Even the
          perches and nests high above are ready. And how's
              (indicating the wire)
          whatever this is going?

Deuce is concentrating on pulling out another wire from the spool.

                    DEUCE CORSICAN
          A few more wires, then connect them all up, attach
          'em, yeah should be done soon.

                         BILL
          Good. Then I guess that all is left is your and Olivia's
          wedding.

Deuce stops, looks up, Olivia shocked too.

                    DEUCE CORSICAN
          What!?!

                         BILL
          Ha! Got ya!

Smiling, Bill leaves. Deuce lets out a breath, but does smile, gets back to his wire work.

                         OLIVIA
              (hopefully)
          Wouldn't be such a bad idea, would it?

Deuce looks at her and smiles.

                    DEUCE CORSICAN
          No, it wouldn't.

Olivia grabs her sack, begins pulling out and inspecting the green tin box structures.

                         OLIVIA
          But, we're not doing it here. We're doing it at the
          barn, got it all figured out and planned.

Deuce looks at her playing his macho bravado, with his shit eating grin.

                    DEUCE CORSICAN
          Ooohhh, so you've been planning this for quite a
          while have ya!?!

                    OLIVIA
          Don't give me that smart ass look!

They concentrate back on their work.

                    DEUCE CORSICAN
          I knew it.

                    OLIVIA
          You knew nothing, ass!

But, he CHUCKLES.

EXT. POLICE MAYOR SYRON'S OUTER GATE, SIDEON - NIGHT

The Guardian pick up from the Barter Exchange road fire fight flies through the gates.

INT. POLICE MAYOR SYRON'S MANSION, BANQUET HALL, SIDEON - NIGHT

Horace and Junior are off away from Syron in a heated debate. Syron is standing
finishing his deer steak by hand. He then drops the steak and plate ONTO the nearby
table.

                    POLICE MAYOR SYRON
          Constance!

He chugs from the wine decanter. Constance appears, cleaning away the food mess on
the table.

A Guardian soldier runs inside the large room and right to Syron. Junior and Horace join
as well.

                    GUARDIAN #8
          The Exchange has been taken!

                    POLICE MAYOR SYRON
          What!?!

                    GUARDIAN #8
          There was a fire fight. There's nobody in the streets.
          They've taken it .

                    POLICE MAYOR SYRON
        Who!?!

                      GUARDIAN #8
              (nervous)
        The people...sir.

Syron grabs the knife from the plate Constance holds and SLASH SLICES the throat of
the Guardian. He drops to floor GURGLING to his death.

                    POLICE MAYOR SYRON
        Horace!

                        HORACE
        I'm on it, sir.

Horace runs out of the Banquet Hall.

                        JUNIOR
        You going to kill everybody?

                    POLICE MAYOR SYRON
        If I have to!

Junior makes that TSK TSK TSK TSK noise from his mouth and tongue.

                        JUNIOR
        You are out of your mind, Father.

                    POLICE MAYOR SYRON
        Watch it, *boy*.

                        JUNIOR
        Your City-State is crumbling around you.

                    POLICE MAYOR SYRON
        This ends now, Junior.

                        JUNIOR
        You are correct. This does end now.

Junior fast draws and BANG! shoots his father in the gut. The absolute surprise on
Syron's face brings a smile to Junior's.

Syron grabs his gut, drops to the floor. Junior looks at the backing up Constance. She
thinks she'll be next.

JUNIOR (CONT'D)
Don't worry, love, I want to keep all of my father's
toys.

He lets her keep backing up. Junior, pure evil and hatred, steps up and stands over his
father.

POLICE MAYOR SYRON
Wh-what is this?

JUNIOR
Regime change.

BANG! A second shot into Syron's leg. Syron GRUNTS in pain, only the shock to his
system prevents him from wailing out. Junior calmly leans down...

POLICE MAYOR SYRON
(struggling)
Burn in hell.

JUNIOR
You first.
(raises the 9mm)

RAY (O.S.)
Junior!

Junior doesn't turn around or shoot, instead he just smiles.

JUNIOR
Damn that sister of mine.

He whips around and FIRES at her, but she ducks back out of the room. He missed.

JUNIOR (CONT'D)
RAY!

He chases after!

Constance slowly walks back to Syron, still alive. He might actually make it if...

POLICE MAYOR SYRON
Constance...thank God. G-go get Doc. I-I need Doc.

Instead Constance grabs the knife from the floor...she squats before him...

                              CONSTANCE
            For seven months you've locked me away here,
            abusing and humiliating me. You thought you had
            control over me.

Syron's expression grows frightful, he's helpless, she's got all the power now.

                              CONSTANCE (CONT'D)
            But, I was a spy. I planted myself here in your inner
            sanctum, spilling all of your secrets and plans. Know
            this as you die, *you* are the reason this Revolution has
            started. And *you* will be the reason your precious
            party and City-State will fail.

She smoothly slides the knife into his gut. He GRUNTS COUGHS not believing what is
happening.

                              CONSTANCE (CONT'D)
            You lost, *Augustus.*

She digs the knife in further...

INT. POLICE MAYOR SYRON'S MANSION, HALLWAY, SIDEON - NIGHT

Roman enters the hallway, slinks in the shadows, slowly heads down the hall, pistol in
hand. A side hallway door opens and he hits the floor, concealed in the darkness!

A Guardian runs off the opposite direction, exits a far door.

INT. POLICE MAYOR SYRON'S MANSION, BANQUET HALL, SIDEON - NIGHT

Ray's back in the Banquet Hall, checks that her father is dead. She instinctively knows
someone is behind the giant couch. She darts around it and finds Constance hiding!

Constance looks up at Ray. This is it. But, she was prepared to die for the cause. Then
something unexpected happens...

                              RAY
            You're free now, Constance.

She can only think of one response.

                              CONSTANCE
            I know.

Roman easily slips inside among the table and chairs on the far side of the Hall to conceal
himself from one of the two side doors. He can't see Constance or Ray behind the couch
from his vantage point.

The front DOORS OPEN.

                    JUNIOR (O.S.)
        RAAAAAYYYY!

Lofted into the air and TUMBLING down the Banquet Hall's floor is the severed head of
a woman! The head slides to the back of the room easily in view of Ray. She and
Constance are frozen in shock as the head settles.

        RAY
    (whispers)
Millie.

                                CONSTANCE
                            (whispers)
                            Millie.

                    JUNIOR
            Come out come out wherever you are! I can do this
            all night! I know you, Ray, you got that weak streak
            in you. You'll want to face me before I kill anyone
            else you know.

Constance stares at the severed head of her friend.

                    CONSTANCE
            (to herself)
        Not Millie.
            (fury grows)
    No.

Constance goes to bolt up, charge and kill Junior. Ray grabs her arm, friendly like, locks
eyes with Constance.

                    RAY
            (low voice)
            Not your kill, Constance. This one's mine.

Constance nods.

EXT. BARTER EXCHANGE, SIDEON - NIGHT

Dallas and his team are continuing setting their numerous land mines. The area is well lit
from hundreds of torches on top of the tin walls and in the ground. Dug holes with the
bricks, nails, and shells are being quickly covered by the loose dirt from the many
wheelbarrows.

The RINGING OF THE BELL!

Everyone outside immediately drop everything and rush back inside the fenced in Barter Exchange. Dallas quickly finishes his last land mine, stands and looks out into the distance...BANG! SPLAT! A bullet finds Dallas, dropping him dead onto the ground!

EXT. BARTER EXCHANGE, TREE LINE, SIDEON - NIGHT

Horace places the rifle back into the saddle bag.

                    FERELL
          Who'd you get?

                    HORACE
          That little traitorous bastard, Dallas.

They get on their motorcycles, REV them to life, put on their helmets.

EXT. BARTER EXCHANGE, SIDEON - NIGHT

Syron's special forces Guardians emerge, Horace and Ferell leading the way, all charging the Exchange on foot, motorcycles, and trucks.

The BARRAGE of GUNFIRE from both sides begins! Moltov cocktails rain down from the high perches inside the Exchange as Syron's forces advance closer.

Horace and Ferell aim their UZIs, steer with one hand as they lead the charge!

Land mines EXPLODE as trucks and motorcycles race over them. They don't do much damaged to the vehicles, except for one, Ferell's motorcycle, whose tire obliterates! Ferell crashes to the ground then is greeted with a Moltov cocktail that engulfs him and his bike into a fireball!

The Guardian forces have reached the front gates and fence! A few foot soldiers are maimed by the homemade land mines, most however are not.

The Battle Siege at the Barter Exchange rages on. Reminiscent of an ancient world invading force trying to storm the castle.

INT. POLICE MAYOR SYRON'S MANSION, BANQUET HALL, SIDEON - NIGHT

BANG! A hostage cook SCREAMS and drops to the floor! Junior advances further inside. BANG! BANG! Fires wildly.

                    RAY
          Stop! What are you doing!?!
               (looks at Millie's severed head)
          What are you doing!?!
               (looks at her father)

Junior smiles at his sister now standing from the couch before him.

                         JUNIOR
            Cleaning house.

He points his gun at the couch.

                         RAY
            Junior stop!

She rushes him! Junior whips the gun over to her! BANG! Ray is dropped to the floor, shot in the upper chest shoulder area. She rolls over on the floor and locks eyes with Roman peeking out from behind a column. They hold their looks...Roman puts his finger to his lips telling her to be quiet. He holds up his pistol, ready to take Junior out.

GUNFIRE ERUPTS outside!

A Guardian barrels inside the Banquet Hall! Junior twirls, takes aim, stopping the Guardian in his tracks.

                         GUARDIAN #9
            We're being attacked!

                         JUNIOR
            Then go deal with it.

BANG! Shoots dangerously close over the Guardian's head.

                         JUNIOR (CONT'D)
         Now!

Ray tries to get up off the floor. Junior calmly walks up to his sister as she desperately crawls and tries to get up.

                         JUNIOR (CONT'D)
                   (taunting her)
            Where you going, Ray???

Exhausted, she rolls back over to her back.

                         RAY
         Why?

Junior stares at her...then that evil smile...

                         JUNIOR
         Why not?

He raises his gun--but catches Roman springing up from behind the column charging at him! Junior FIRES! Roman FIRES! Junior's misses, Roman's bullet shatters Junior's wrist! Roman launches, body tackling SLAMMING Junior to the floor!

EXT. BARTER EXCHANGE, INNER GROUNDS, SIDEON - NIGHT

The battle rages on! The Barter Exchange tin wall fences slowly being battered down. Deuce runs through chaos.

> DEUCE CORSICAN
> GRENADES! GRENADES!

The men on the perches begin lobbing down Deuce's homemade grenades. EXPLOSIONS after EXPLOSIONS!!

EXT. BARTER EXCHANGE, SIDEON - NIGHT

The grenades, Moltov Cocktails and gunfire do damage on the advancing forces. They're stuck not able to break through and inside the Exchange.

A RUMBLING SOUND shakes the earth. The men outside stop and look.

EXT. BARTER EXCHANGE, INNER GROUNDS, SIDEON - NIGHT

The RUMBLING SOUND shaking the premises stop the fighters inside as well. Deuce looks up to one of the perches at the fence.

> DEUCE CORSICAN
> WHAT IS THAT!?!

EXT. BARTER EXCHANGE, SIDEON - NIGHT

Emerging from the darkness...a behemoth, tank like monster on wheels! A rugged steel box structured vehicle infested with barbwire and spikes jutting out. Its heading right for the front gates!

EXT. BARTER EXCHANGE, INNER GROUNDS, SIDEON - NIGHT

The fighter up high on the perch calls down to Deuce.

> FIGHTER
> A METAL MONSTER! IT'S GONNA RAM
> THROUGH! NO STOPPING IT!

INT. POLICE MAYOR SYRON'S MANSION, BANQUET HALL, SIDEON - NIGHT

Roman scrambles for his pistol, Junior, cradling his gunshot wounded wrist, picks his pistol and himself up off the floor. He FIRES! But, Roman isn't there!

Two Guardians rush inside!

> GUARDIAN #9
> They've breached the perimeter!

Junior turns to kill his sister! But, she has just crawled dragged herself back behind the couch and out of temporary sight. Junior turns back to the soldiers.

JUNIOR
Burn it! And everyone inside!

Junior runs to the front doors. Roman leaps out from behind a column and OPENS FIRE! Junior throws a Guardian in the bullet's path, killing him! Roman FIRES again as Junior reaches the door, the bullet SMACKS into his back by the ribs flinging Junior off his feet and out the Banquet Hall's front door!

The second Guardian FIRES back at Roman, who isn't there! Then BANG! Roman drops the second Guardian dead on the floor.

INT. POLICE MAYOR SYRON'S MANSION, BANQUET HALL ENTRYWAY, SIDEON - NIGHT

Roman walks to Junior just out the doors on the floor. Junior is damaged beyond repair yet his free hand and arm are struggling to find anything to grab. Its HARD for him TO BREATHE. Roman walks right to him and SHOOTS him in the back of the head. He run back to Ray.

INT. POLICE MAYOR SYRON'S MANSION, BANQUET HALL, SIDEON - NIGHT

Roman reaches to Ray. Their eyes lock yet again...Roman acts, Ray flinches, but he instead moves to help her and her wound.

ROMAN
Need to stop the bleeding.

Ray is so confused.

ROMAN (CONT'D)
Hey! I'm here to help you! You need to dress the wound!

RAY
Junior?

ROMAN
I got him for you.

RAY
Th-th-the box.

But, she's talking to Constance. Roman whips around to find her standing there.

                         ROMAN
          Hey Constance.

                       CONSTANCE
          I was wondering when my favorite uncle was going
          to show up.

                         ROMAN
          I'm your only uncle.

Roman springs up to the curtains and RIPS them down as Constance runs out the side
door to the kitchen. He uses the curtains to help stop the bleeding.

Constance returns, hands over the box to Roman.

                          RAY
          The clear...Bottle.
                  (he grabs it)
          Pou-our it over.
                  (musters strength)
          Pour it!

Roman does. The liquid hits the wound and Ray SCREAMS!

                       CONSTANCE
          I need to help the staff. Meet me at the back
          gatehouse.

                         ROMAN
          Be safe.

Roman TEARS strips from the curtain, wraps Ray's shoulder which produces much pain
for her.

An EXPLOSION ROCKS the Banquet Hall! Then a Moltov Cocktail EXPLODES
inside! Flames catch and spread!

Marcus and two of Marcus' fighters race inside!

                   MARKUS CORSICAN (O.S.)
          Roman!?!

                         ROMAN
          Here!

Roman gets in front of Ray as the two fighters and Marcus appear. GUNFIRE ERUPTS,
more EXPLOSIONS

ROMAN (CONT'D)
Do what you came here to do! I'm good!

The fighters run off. Roman turns to Ray.

ROMAN (CONT'D)
I need to get you out of here.

Ray shakes her head. She's done.

RAY
No. Leave me be.

EXT. BARTER EXCHANGE, SIDEON - NIGHT

The metal monster RAMS the front gates of the Barter Exchange! Slowly the behemoth strains the tin wall fence and gates down.

Grenades and Molotov Cocktails rain down and EXPLODE onto the tank vehicle! The metal monster motors onward.

INT. BARTER EXCHANGE, INNER GROUNDS, SIDEON - NIGHT

Deuce runs to the WWII style air raid horn. He cranks the handle over and over again. EEERRRRRRRR! EEERRRRRR! EEERRRRRR! The fighters know the warning, spring into action!

They all run for the back to escape! It's weird, they seem to be jump hurdling every so often in intervals as they race away from the fight and out the back!

HORACE (O.S.)
THEY'RE RETREATING! RETREATING!
CHARGE!

EXT. POLICE MAYOR SYRON'S MANSION, FRONT, SIDEON - NIGHT

This mini battle rages on between Markus' fighters and the Guardian soldiers.

EXT. POLICE MAYOR SYRON'S MANSION, BACK, SIDEON - NIGHT

Roman, with his arm around Ray's waist, cradle runs her and himself out and through the grounds to the back gate house. A pick up truck barrels down on them. There's nothing they can do.

RAY
Go. Leave me. You can get out.

Roman looks at her...then back at the oncoming truck.

                    ROMAN
        Nah. Think I hang for a bit.

                    RAY
        Can we sit, then?
            (lets a smile escape)

They do.

                    RAY (CONT'D)
        You're an idiot. You know that right?

                    ROMAN
        I do.

The truck reaches them, the driver jumps out. It's Markus!

                    MARKUS CORSICAN
        What the hell!?!

He recognizes Ray, pulls his pistol!

                    ROMAN
        No! She's with me.

More EXPLOSIONS and GUNFIRE! Markus lowers his weapon.

                    ROMAN (CONT'D)
        You seen Constance?

                    MARKUS CORSICAN
        Gate house with the staff! Take the truck. I got
        business to tend to. Go!

Markus runs off. Ray looks at Roman.

                    RAY
        What's going on?

                    ROMAN
        I don't know.

                    RAY
        What do we do?

                    ROMAN
        Get the hell out of here.

EXT. BARTER EXCHANGE, SIDEON - NIGHT

The metal monster GRINDS and BENDS the front gates and tin wall fence down just enough for the foot soldiers to get through. The monster FORCES forward CRASHING the gates and fence down! The Guardian soldiers, Horace, motorcycles, and pick ups storm the grounds!

INT. BARTER EXCHANGE, INNER GROUNDS, SIDEON - NIGHT

Syron's forces rampage inside but all the living fighters are gone.

> HORACE
> They went out the back!

Led by the running Horace, the forces advance towards the back of the Exchange.

Legs, motorcycles, and trucks all trip the numerous wires strung about the premises. That's why the fighters were jumping when fleeing the Exchange. Its a trap! And its too late.

WHOOSH! WHOOSH! SNAP! BANG! WHOOSH! CLICK! The impressive series of trip wires engage then ignite Olivia's and Deuce's planted explosives all around and inside the Exchange!

> HORACE (CONT'D)
> (realizing)
> Shit.

EXT. PASTURE LANDS, SIDEON - NIGHT

Deuce, Olivia, Bill, Riley and the rest of the survivors stop and turn as the MASSIVE MULTIPLE EXPLOSIONS ERUPT! A once in a lifetime fireworks explosion display! The group CHEERS as the Barter Exchange amasses into one giant fireball!

> DEUCE CORSICAN
> Ok!
> (he kisses Olivia on the cheek)
> Ok. On the move people. On the move.

We watch the fire and smoke billow into the sky as we...

FADE OUT:

EXT. POLICE MAYOR SYRON'S MANSION PROPERTY, SIDEON - NIGHT

The remnants of this battle. Guardians dead all around, most of Markus' team dead on the grounds as well...

                    KYRA (V.O.)
        We sacrificed in our own blood for the chance to be
        free, to survive...

INT. POLICE MAYOR SYRON'S MANSION, BANQUET HALL, SIDEON - NIGHT

...we see Syron dead on the floor...

                    KYRA (V.O.)
        We stopped the Evil at its core...

EXT. REVOLUTIONARIES ENCAMPMENT, BORDERLANDS - NIGHT

The headlights of the vehicles are spread out in front of the encampment. Dykes and
Manus lead the band of Dweller fighters out from the brush to the beginning of the camp.

Nestled tightly are a dozen or so huge army tents, all filled with Revolutionaries. Dykes
smiles.

                    DYKES
        Do your damage.

Manus smiles. Lifts his barbwire rebarb infested spike high and WAR CRIES. The
Dwellers follow suit and ECHO the WAR CRY and all charge the tents. Dykes keeps
walking forward wanting to see the carnage.

The Dwellers attack! They destroy tent after tent after...there are no people...anywhere.
Place is empty. No food, no materials, no people.

Dykes smile fades...

The Dwellers amass around Manus, who turns to face Dykes. It's Manus' turn to grin
then WAR CRY SCREAM. He points his barbwire rebarb infested spike directly at
Dykes. They charge. Dykes tries to turn and out run them, but the Dwellers are on him
before he can. Dykes' death won't be pretty.

EXT. BARTER EXCHANGE, INNER GROUNDS, SIDEON - MORNING

Syron's forces are all destroyed, burnt reminders from the carcass of the once busy Barter
Exchange from the battle...

                    KYRA (V.O.)
        But not forever...

A MOTOR STARTS...

The burnt metal monster COMES TO LIFE, BARELY, and begins its difficult task of
backing its way out of the Exchange...

                         KYRA (V.O.) (CONT'D)
            Those who seek complete power will be difficult to
            defeat. It will always be a constant threat. In our
            world, armies will always be forged to support the
            next tyrannical leader. But, we gave our Warlord and
            that system one hell of a crushing blow...

EXT. CORISCAN BROTHERS' BARN, BORDERLANDS - MORNING

The people are eating a joyous breakfast among the multiple campfires. Two pick up
trucks pull into the camp. Deuce and Olivia go out to meet.

Markus and three soldiers get out of one vehicle. Markus and Deuce embrace. Roman,
Constance, and Syron's house staff of four exit the other.

                         KYRA (V.O.)
            We believe the forces of Good will always prevail.
            No matter the costs or the odds...

Roman hugs his niece, Constance wipes away a tear. He smiles and nods as he back
steps to the pick up truck. He waves a final time to her, Deuce, Markus, and the rest as
he gets in and drives off.

EXT. CORISCAN BROTHERS' BARN, BORDERLANDS - DAY

Deuce and Olivia kiss in front of Bill holding a bible...the first time as husband and wife.

                         KYRA (V.O.)
            ...because the freedom to love, to choose, to pursue
            happiness is always worth dying for.

Deuce and Olivia hold their locked hands into the air, Deuce loving it and playing it to
those in attendance, Olivia smilingly can't take her eyes off of him. They walk back
down the aisle to the cheers of the crowd. Deuce can't help but scoop his woman up and
carry her the rest of the way.

Markus rolls his eyes and Riley elbows him in the side. They lock eyes and can't help but
smile too. She links her arm into his and they follow the new couple back down the aisle.

                                                                FADE OUT:

FADE IN:

EXT. BORDERLANDS, WOODS - MORNING

Roman walks through the woods with a pan full of freshly picked berries.

                    KYRA (V.O.)
          And as for the story of my father...

ON Roman as he grins when he walks up on the pick up truck and to the opened
passenger side door.

                  KYRA (V.O.) (CONT'D)
          ...and my mother...

Ray, comfortably stretched out in the cab, her wound freshly and cleanly dressed
wrapped in white bandages, smiles at Roman when he appears.

                        RAY
          Mmmm. Berries again? You sure know how to
          impress a lady.

Roman smiles and hand feeds her the first of many.

                    KYRA (V.O.)
          ...well, that's a whole nother story.

                      THE END